We all have quests in life.

WebQuests

WebQuests

TESOL Strategy Guide

DAVID KENT

Pedagogy Press

National Library of Australia Cataloguing-in-Publication entry:
Kent, David Bradley, author.
Webquests / David Kent.

ISBN: 9781925555073 (paperback) (4)
TESOL strategy guide ; 4.
Includes bibliographical references.
Teachers of English to Speakers of Other Languages.
Educational technology.
Teaching—Aids and devices.
Teachers—Training of.
Internet in education.
English language—Study and teaching—Foreign speakers.

Pedagogy Press. Sydney, Australia.
www.pedagogypress.com

First Edition.

For teachers everywhere.

CONTENTS

Preface

This *TESOL Strategy Guide,* number four in the set, arose out of the clear need to provide teacher training and a means of professional development to educators living and working in the Republic of Korea. Many expatriate English language instructors have arrived in-country without training as a teacher or educator, and are often left to take care of their own professional development while engaged in teaching English to speakers of other languages (TESOL). As many of these teachers come to enjoy working as expatriates, they often begin to seek out their own professional development on topics that they wish to learn more about, on skills that they wish to gain, and on techniques that they wish to integrate within their classrooms. It is this need, which is common to all teachers of English in all contexts around the globe, that this book seeks to fill.

Organization of the text

Each *TESOL Strategy Guide* can be read standalone or in conjunction with others from the set. Each book provides information on a technology topic, and has been designed around a question-based format similar to the following:

- Overview
- What is … ?
- How can I use … ?
- What types of … exist?
- What elements are behind an effective … ?
- How can … lend itself to TESOL?
- How can I start using … with students?
- How do I evaluate a … ?
- What tools are available for … creation?
- How do I craft a … ?
- How would I use a tool to create a … ?
- What are the key points behind … use in the TESOL context?

A comprehensive list of resources with links to pertinent web sites and applications is included, along with lesson plan guides, example implementation techniques, and various free to use handouts for the teacher and student alike. A reference list of all works cited also allows those teachers with an interest in a particular topic to engage in reading further on the issues that most interest them and impact their learners.

It is hoped that this book will provide both education and something new for all teachers – be they trained or untrained, pre-service, in-service, seasoned, or retired.

1

Overview

This book focuses on the use and applicability of the WebQuests in the 21st century educational environment, particularly as they relate to the teaching of English to speakers of other languages (TESOL). With the need to develop and foster multiple literacies in our students today, the WebQuest model is as relevant now as it was at the dawn of the internet. To this end, aspects of the model best suited to the TESOL context are provided, with the learning theory behind the development of the WebQuest model covered in detail. The type of WebQuests that are available and the topics best suited to WebQuest creation are also covered, along with effective development techniques, the types of WebQuests, and the benefits and adaptability of using the model with TESOL students is explored. This is augmented by the provision of various evaluation strategies for assessing self-created and pre-developed WebQuests, and for assessing any WebQuest that students complete during class. The tools and templates to develop a WebQuest for classroom use are then highlighted, with a practitioner guide to this process arising from the included material that is useable as classroom content, with a number of photocopiable handouts that go along with it. This is further supported by a wide variety of additional resources to assist in the use and development of WebQuests for the classroom.

2

What is a WebQuest?

Dr. Bernie Dodge, as professor of Educational Technology at San Diego State University, is the originator of the WebQuest model which was developed in the mid-1990s with contributions from Tom March, Educational Technology staff of the San Diego Unified School District (Dodge, 2015). Since that time, and with the growth of the internet, many teachers have been able to employ this model, developing their own WebQuests that they used with their students, and then made freely available for other educators to download.

Like the models used to develop lesson plans, the WebQuest model, although now over two decades old, still holds its own as an inquiry-oriented learning tool. As opposed to the 'traditional' model of learning, relying on mastery of skills and an empty vessel approach with a 'sage on the stage', inquiry-oriented learning focuses more on using and learning content in order to develop skills such as problem-solving or information processing. Inquiry-based learning, combined with technology models in the EFL context, has led to an improvement in student linguistic skills, increased the development of social skills, the learning of different cultural aspects, and to gains in wider perspectives on topics (Arauz, 2013).

Ultimately, there are five distinguishing characteristics of a WebQuest (EBC, 2004). First, Webquests are classroom-based lessons where all or most of the information that students explore and evaluate comes from the internet. Second, emphasis is placed on the development of analysis, promotion of creativity, criticism, and other higher-order thinking skills, over that of simply information gathering. Third, as all of the internet sources are teacher-selected and -presented, the tasks are heavily teacher-guided but remain student-centered with an emphasis on information use. Fourth, students are intended to take on various roles as part of a WebQuest. And fifth, WebQuests are usually group-oriented.

As such, WebQuests offer the following to students of instructors that are teaching English to speakers of other languages (TESOL):

- A means to utilize all that the internet has to offer, but in a controlled manner.
- Present teacher-directed and -developed content that leads to intensively student-focused lessons.
- Provide teaching material that promotes learner autonomy by requiring students to use, rely on, and develop their own skills as they work through the presented learning content together.
- Ensure that learners gain access to authentic language and learning content from within a technology-rich framework.
- Establish a learning environment where students can begin to focus on using language collaboratively to process information as well as engage in problem solving activities.

3

How can I use WebQuests?

WebQuests are classroom-based lessons where all or most of the information that students explore and evaluate is internet-based. They emphasize higher-order thinking, and are teacher-guided but student-centered, with information use and understanding developed from role-based involvement with learning content that enables students to then work out a conclusion or answer to the set task(s) or problem(s). These lessons are classroom-based and each can be incorporated into a 50-minute single lesson used as a once-off, developed for use as part of a month long unit, or incorporated into the curriculum for an entire semester. WebQuests can be used to promote learning and motivation while employing constructivism, situated learning, and inquiry-based learning principles.

The key behind the successful development and use of a WebQuest is to use the internet to provide motivating learning material in the form of an authentic task, and present this material to students using a scaffolded learning approach which is based on constructivism and situated learning that they must then take on board to complete by taking on roles and participating in an inquiry-based method of learning (March, 2004).

Motivating Tasks

From the outset, any WebQuest task needs to be designed to motivate learners to want to learn or begin a quest of discovery using the materials and roles provided by the WebQuest itself. Tasks need to be built upon internet-based material that provides some level of interactivity, are media dense, contain different perspectives, and are tailored to the teaching and learning context of students. In this way, WebQuests can begin to offer more than textbooks, photocopiable handouts, or activity-based worksheets, and provide motivation for learners to engage with the content and to begin to challenge their own perspectives.

Tasks therefore rely on authentic content to be completed successfully, and lead students to develop knowledge and participate in learning through contextualization based on a socio-constructivist model of scaffolded learning.

Scaffolding

Scaffolding can be built into a good WebQuest by providing partly completed tasks, and by finding the best resources for participants to work out how to complete them. Learners then use this content to form their background understanding, or build upon existing schema, before they begin to engage with more specific resources targeting their specialized role in the WebQuest. Scaffolding thereby provides learners with the opportunity to contextualize content knowledge and engage in situated learning (Pederson, 2013; Chou, 2014). This method allows for teachers to think about teaching differently. WebQuests provide a means for the teacher to move from being a 'sage on the stage' to a 'guide on the side' during lesson time, and even though the content and material is extremely teacher-provided, the activities are student–centered. Learners engage with the material and employ the content during class time to build their own knowledge and develop their own personal meanings and understandings of the content before coming together to make sense of it. It is this deep understanding, developed from scaffolded knowledge, that is then presented to the teacher for evaluation. In order to do this successfully, students must provide each other with assistance to socially negotiate meaning. They can do this by exchanging resources with each other, and by offering each other feedback. It is also in this way that individuals can be held accountable for their own learning, as well as the learning development of others.

Questioning

Any question that can be answered 'yes' or 'no', or is able to be answered by cutting and pasting, is not suitable for inclusion in a good WebQuest. Questions must be those that students can answer directly via investigation or by engaging in inquiry. Good WebQuest questions are also those that take into account students current academic and language skill levels, as well as the relevant prior knowledge that might be required of the WebQuest overall.

The questions must promote critical thinking skills. In other words, questions must ensure that students need to do more than participate in information gathering activities. Students should be able to examine the information collated, and process it to form their own opinions about the topic or subject matter. WebQuests primarily achieve this by assigning specific roles to individuals or specific group members, and therefore these individuals or groups then have their own research agenda to carry out, and this must then be discussed and presented to all group members to resolve the overall problem, situation, or task presented as the main WebQuest end goal.

Answers must not be already known
"What is K-pop?" is a little too straightforward for a WebQuest. "What musical styles does K-Pop draw from, and how is this represented on stage and in

music videos?" offers a much wider opportunity for research and exploration.

Answers must not be simple facts

"In what year did the Korean War start?" can be looked up very easily online, can be asked of a friend or relative, or may already be known. "What factors led to the start of the Korean War?" is a better question, as it requires research, interpretation, and analysis.

Answers should not be too personal

"Why do you like K-Pop?" can lead to internalization and to thinking about the self. "What have people said about K-Pop recently?" would see students research the question based on gender, or other demographics such as age.

Answers must contain an objective basis

"Does long term sun exposure cause skin cancer?" calls for a value judgment, whereas "What does the evidence suggest is the cause of skin cancer?" calls for research.

Answers must be answerable

"What factors have led the song *arirang* to become representative of Korea?" is answerable, perhaps many ways, whereas "Why was the fourth word of the second line of the song *arirang* chosen by the composer?" could not be answered with any certainty.

Ultimately, WebQuests can be used in the classroom for knowledge acquisition and integration, as well as extending and defining the depth of student knowledge. As such, WebQuests can be used to close off a topic as a review piece in the short-term. They can also lead into longer-term portfolio pieces to be used for grading and for demonstrations of meeting standards, and to provide take-home material for stakeholders such as parents, administration, and even the learners themselves. This leads us into the two types of WebQuests.

4

What are the two types of WebQuest?

The two types of WebQuest are short-term and long-term, and each has its own goal.

Type One – The short-term WebQuest

The goal of the short-term WebQuest is knowledge acquisition and integration where the learner engages with a significant amount of new information, and comes to make sense of it. The short-term WebQuest would only ever cover one to three class periods. It is useful to consolidate skills, such as a need to develop a book trailer based on a class assigned novel after completing a digital storytelling unit.

Other good examples of short-term WebQuests involve students working in teams that require them to take on immediate roles to solve a problem, such as determining the reasons behind the death of a King or the substantiation of the rumor that Mozart was murdered by a rival composer (Benjamin, 2003).

Type Two – The long-term WebQuest

The goal of the long-term WebQuest is to extend and define knowledge. The learner is expected to deeply analyze the body of available knowledge, and create something to which others can respond. The long-term WebQuest might cover from one week to one month of class time, and it also provides an opportunity to create portfolio projects and the assessment of group skills longitudinally, while simultaneously being able to provide a demonstrable outcome that can be shared with other stakeholders (such as student peers, parents, and administration).

The challenge with a long-term WebQuest is that it needs to sustain student interest. Such WebQuests will also typically need to meet several standards if used in a school setting, and might therefore need to include interdisciplinary work. An example might be to create an itinerary for a family group visiting Korea where investigation of the people, climate, economy, culture, customs, available leisure activities, cuisine, and the physical geography of the nation are all likely to be taken into account. Investigating each of these areas supports a broad range of disciplines (for example, history, geography, sports, mathematics, and culinary arts). Multi-literacies are also supported when gathering country specific information from different kinds of text (for example, books, articles, and brochures) and interpreting data when listening to and watching various media types (for example, documentaries on the one hand and contemporary music videos on the other). Digital literacies are further addressed when using technology as a means to cohesively tie the information together.

Whatever the length of the WebQuest, the ultimate goal is to see learners enjoy the undertaking and participation in projects, and to ultimately help develop within them aspects of learner autonomy and the ability to undertake research. This is achieved particularly when students actively engage in group discussions when exploring a central issue, and develop the necessary searching and critical thinking skills to examine the information sources that are presented to them. For second-language learners, the opportunity for linguistic development also arises when they use the target language for reading information, listening to audio materials, and watching videos relating to the WebQuest topic, then writing presentations and listening to peers' opinions and ideas when discussing the critical issues that relate to the topic and the final outcome of the WebQuest.

5

What elements are behind an effective WebQuest layout?

There is a set WebQuest format which serves well as a guide to follow when beginning to construct a WebQuest for students (EBC, 2004). Becoming familiar with this layout will also help in thinking through some of the key elements behind WebQuest development when it comes time to develop one of your own, or assessing the use of one designed by another teacher for use with your students.

The layout involves an introduction or description, statement of the task itself, the process required to complete the task, resources required while engaging in the process, the evaluation method used by the teacher, and a means of conclusion or presentation of the completed task.

Introduction

Establish clear and concise background information, learning goals, and motivational scenarios that engage students (for example, "You are an astronaut going to the moon."). Include the reasons why the topic is one worthy of investigating.

Task

Set an interesting and concrete central task, and provide a formal description of what students will have accomplished by the end of the WebQuest. The task is the focus for the learners' activities, so consider those that are motivating, inspirational, and potentially fun to engage in.

Process

This is the section of the WebQuest where you provide a description of all the steps that learners should go through in order to accomplish the task. The roles of each group member need to be made very clear in this step. Include guidance and support, and potentially tips on how to divide responsibilities amongst students, or how to find and organize the information or resources that will be collated for analysis. Any description of roles and responsibilities should be offered together with scaffolding tools (like handouts and templates).

Resources

Resources are all the items that students will need to complete the task, and include bookmarked websites, print resources, and online multimedia sources. Resources can also extend to include non-web-based content such as audio/video as well as field trips to locations such as museums. This can be a separate section, or the resources can be presented on an as-needed basis throughout the 'Process' section. It is now encouraged by Dodge (2016) to include the necessary elements from the resources section in the process section as they are required in a fully developed and completed WebQuest. However, in the early developmental stages of a WebQuest when it is being created by a teacher, it may prove easier to keep these sections separated so that each section of the layout has a single process that needs focusing upon at the time it is being written up. Essentially, as WebQuests provide all relevant links to students as they are designed to extremely efficient and focused lessons that can prevent students from wandering around the internet and going off-task. All material should be pre-selected by the teacher.

Evaluation

Each WebQuest needs an evaluation rubric, with fair, clear, consistent, and specific components relative to the tasks set. Further details on development and inclusion of a rubric for WebQuest assessment are discussed later in this book.

Conclusion

There are two elements of this section: reflection by students, and a summary of the goals and achievements provided by completing the WebQuest presented by the teacher. Time should also be set aside to discuss any potential points of interest or elements of application emerging from the student reflection session. Typical final projects presented in conclusion might consist of oral presentations as well as presentations based on written materials (for example, brochure development, newsletter creation, or blog and wiki development).

6

How do WebQuests lend themselves to TESOL?

WebQuests offer several benefits to second-language learners of English, including:

1. They provide exposure to a significant amount of authentic language, primarily when engaging in the reading of texts for task completion, but also when processing any included streaming media (audio- or video-based).

2. They develop co-operation skills in students. Students who work together to complete tasks and roles can enhance their communicative opportunities and in turn their linguistic abilities through language practice.

3. They can encourage motivation and learner engagement. This is achieved if they are developed with an appropriate hook, and they appeal to students interests.

4. They provide support for several learning methods. Constructivist learning theory is

supported through the use of scaffolding and learning from a zone of proximal development (ZPD). Students engage with the development of knowledge through a situational learning context driven by inquiry-based learning methods.

For WebQuests, focus is often placed on the reading of material for task and role completion, and in turn the writing up of this information for presentation. In the TESOL context in this regard, WebQuests have been used to support the development of reading and writing opportunities for students, especially for developing critical reading skills, with Ahmad (2012) seeing that WebQuests are useful for this purpose among college level students of English as a foreign language (EFL). Alshumaimeri and Almasri (2012) also view WebQuests as beneficial for developing the reading skills of students, particularly for increasing comprehension skills. However, they also warn that teachers and students need to be trained or fully understand how to go about delivering and conducting a WebQuest in order to gain full benefit from the use of this model.

Other benefits that have emerged for second-language learners using WebQuests see apprehension of writing reduced and writing performance enhanced (Chuo, 2007), while simultaneously providing authentic learning materials and collaborative tasks (Kocoglu, 2010). Zlatkovska (2010) also recognizes that WebQuests provide a more student-centered and constructivist model of teaching, which facilitates English language teaching and technology integration as part of non-native speaker English teacher training.

An important aspect to consider when using an existing WebQuest is its suitability for the TESOL context. In this regard, as Prapinwong and Puthikanon (2008) remind us, five factors are important to take into account, and these include the vocabulary and grammar levels of students, along with their prior knowledge, the interestingness provided by the WebQuest, and the amount of assistance/scaffolding provided to the learner to complete the tasks. Assessing the potential use or modification of a WebQuest is always important, as it is with any learning material developed by another teacher for use with your own students and teaching style.

7

What topics are suitable for WebQuests?

Webquests can be applied to a range of topics, but not all. The topics that they are most suitable for involve tasks that require creativity, and have problems with several possible solutions.

WebQuests can address open-ended questions like:
- What should be done to protect Australia's Great Barrier Reef?
- What can be done to save what's left of the Amazon rainforest?
- What was it like to live during the Australian gold rush?
- What was it like to live in Korea under Japanese colonial rule?

For students of a lower language level, like second-language learners and young learners, the following roles may be more appropriate.
- Book reviewer: working as a member of a team to develop a trailer for an upcoming book

launch. This lends itself to any book, and any level of student.

- Reporter: working as a member of a team to produce a magazine section consisting of several articles. Topics of the section can be broad, and focus on travel, cuisine, or important cultural events.

- Investigator: working as a member of an elite police squad investigating all of the clues assigned to a particular role (beat detective, crime scene investigator, medical examiner) to solve a murder mystery.

- Travel agent: investigate the economy, leisure activities, accommodations, and cuisine of a certain country or group of countries for a one month family vacation and to be included in a travel brochure.

For the TESOL context overall, the tasks or roles set by the WebQuest should encourage use of the target language. For example, gathering information from written resources provides learners with reading practice, after which, the information acquired can be discussed in groups before then being put into practice (by perhaps developing a brochure). Tasks should also promote collaboration and meaningful communication amongst students, with the material presented for use being not only authentic but which they would likely use or come across in their daily lives (Koenraad & Westhoff, 2003).

8

How do I evaluate WebQuests?

Perhaps the most appropriate means available to evaluate pre-existing and self-created WebQuests, particularly for use in the TESOL context, is to use a prefabricated rubric based upon a Likert-type rating scale. Similar rubrics can also be applied to the work that students produce after completing a WebQuest. In this case, any such rubric should be presented to students beforehand, so that they can understand what will be assessed and expected from them.

Evaluation rubrics, particularly those using indicators across several categories, are essential when assessing the quality of WebQuests that are freely available for download, but even those that are well-developed they may have been created for slightly different teaching contexts than yours. While it is useful for the busy teacher to apply pre-made rubrics it is even better if teacher to formulate ones of their own that reflect their specific teaching environment and the points that they wish to assess. One good source for this is Rubistar, where there are a number of pre-made evaluation options as well as information on how to create unique context sensitive evaluation instruments. The rubrics section of the resources list also contains several other rubric creation tools that may prove worthwhile to look over.

The rating scale used in the following rubrics goes from 1 to 5, with 1 being poor, 2 fair, 3 average, 4 good, and 5 excellent. 'Average' is used as a midpoint so that students can see how each particular skill relates to peers. This allows teachers to identify those skills that are weak in individual students, and those that may need improvement.

Pre-Developed/Self-Created WebQuest

Assessment Item	Assessment Criteria	Score
Introduction	Relates to learner interests; describes a compelling question or problem.	1 2 3 4 5
Task	Engaging, and elicits thinking that goes beyond rote comprehension.	1 2 3 4 5
Processes	Different roles are assigned to help students share responsibility in accomplishing the task.	1 2 3 4 5
Resources	There is a clear and meaningful connection between resources and the required information.	1 2 3 4 5
Evaluation	The criteria for success are clear, with the evaluation instrument measuring what students must know and be able to do when the WebQuest is complete.	1 2 3 4 5

Ratings: 1 Poor 2 Fair 3 Average 4 Good 5 Excellent

Student Completed WebQuest

Assessment Item	Assessment Criteria	Score
Introduction	Questions answered completely, with clear and sound rationale behind the answers.	1 2 3 4 5
Task	The task is completed, and the means of completing the task, or the plan followed to achieve it, is well executed.	1 2 3 4 5
Processes	Students clearly worked well as a team, with the final product a result of equal collaboration amongst all members.	1 2 3 4 5
Resources	Ideas expressed are based on the resources provided, but demonstrate originality.	1 2 3 4 5
Evaluation and Conclusion	Students were able to achieve the final goal of the WebQuest, with the final presented work substantially free of language errors such as grammar and spelling, and with the expected formatting or presentation method followed.	1 2 3 4 5

Ratings: 1 Poor 2 Fair 3 Average 4 Good 5 Excellent

9

What tools are available for WebQuest creation?

There is no specific software tool available to develop a WebQuest. However, there are a number of templates available and a number of websites and applications that will use a software-based template and present a model to help you develop a WebQuest in the correct format. These websites can be found in the resources list, under WebQuest, and two template-driven sites are discussed in more detail a little later in this book.

The rudimentary template that is followed when creating a WebQuest has the following:
- Introduction – orients and captures interest
- Task – presents the required end goal
- Process – details steps to achieve the end goal
- Resources – provides materials for the task
- Evaluation – measures the results
- Conclusion – presents the results

Aspects of the above components need to be crafted by the individual teacher as they go. Keep in mind that WebQuests are designed to use student time efficiently, as students are using the links to resource material provided and are not out searching for it. When accessing such content, students also need to rely on higher order thinking skills (analysis, synthesis, and evaluation techniques) to engage with it effectively. As a result, Dodge (2001), has determined that *focus* is pivotal to the creation of a good WebQuest, that is: *f*inding excellent sites, *o*rchestrating learners and resources, *c*hallenging thinking in learners, *u*sing mediums to advantage, and *s*caffolding great expectations.

Finding excellent sites

Assess sites for authenticity to task, interestingness to students, relevancy for language learning, and for content that is up-to-date.

Orchestrating learners and resources

Establish tasks and processes that guide learners to be cooperative, collaborative, accountable, and reflect upon their work, and that require a need to share information between all members of the team so that only in this way can the task actually be accomplished.

Judiciously use and apply all the materials that you have access to from your teaching and learning context (both physical and virtually accessible); that is, develop offline and online lesson components to accommodate the teaching and learning context as necessary.

Challenging thinking in learners

Learner is no longer simply about the memorization of information and facts; students today need to be able to work in teams and collaborate on projects. Creativity and imagination needs to be developed alongside critical thinking and problem solving abilities, and these need to be incorporated into any classroom content that students engage with for learning and for communicating. Multi-literacy skills (including information literacy, media literacy, and technology literacy) are also increasingly being emphasized, along with social and cross-cultural skills, and traits leading to adaptability and flexibility, productivity and accountability, initiative and self-direction, as well as leadership and responsibility.

The task set by the WebQuest needs to accommodate the development of these skills and traits, and it is recognized that the task is the key component to successful WebQuest design. Tasks must go beyond retelling, and they should engage students in the development of the essential skills and traits that they will need to succeed as 21st century learners.

Using mediums to advantage

The pedagogogical structure of a WebQuest lends itself to several different media, not just static web pages and links to newspaper articles. Links can be to videos, podcasts, infographics, social media, or even some offline content. However, a WebQuest that can be done completely offline does not exploit the digital or technological media that is available to teachers and students today, and is simply no more than a worksheet-based activity that might contain some internet links.

Scaffolding great expectations

Scaffolding learning through the selection of various resources and task requirements allows learners to build upon previous schema and to work together to develop content that they may not otherwise have been able to produce.

There are three kinds of scaffolding commonly employed in a WebQuest: reception, transformation, and production (Dodge, 2001). The reception aspect puts students in contact with resources that they may not have chosen or used before, and requires a level of guidance to be incorporated into the process of making meaning or learning from the content. Types of this content might include guides, tips, glossaries, or a thesaurus. The transformation aspect requires students to change what they read, see, hear, or experience into a new form of knowledge.; for example recognizing a pattern in data, finding comparisons or contrasts across several media elements, engaging in brainstorming, participating in decision making, or conducting inductive reasoning. Essentially, the production aspect will see students develop or create something that did not previously exist. To complete such tasks, the use of templates, prompted writing guides, and various multimedia elements is imperative. Example end products include something as complex as a cookbook that consists of various culturally-based recipes, a magazine consisting of various articles, and the development of a three minute book trailer or a yearly highlights reel.

10

How do I craft a WebQuest?

To begin to develop a WebQuest, it's a good idea to focus on each section one at a time.

Introduction/Description

Introduce the WebQuest to students by writing the WebQuest with the students as the audience. Provide an overview, and set up any role-playing scenarios in this section. In other words, this section should be used to prepare the students for the tasks that they need to undertake, and provide an overview of the lesson and activities. To capture student interest regarding the topic, use a motivational 'hook' or a captivating question.

Task

This is where you will state the end results of students' activities by informing them of what tasks they must achieve by the end of the Webquest.

Tasks might be comprised of elements such as

- a series of questions,
- a number of problems that require solving, or
- sides of an argument that must be formulated and then defended.

Keep in mind that tasks need to focus on students' being able to work with the material to gain an understanding of the arguments and positions, and then formulate their own opinion and understanding of the topic.

Process

In this section, list a step-by-step process for students to follow when completing the assigned task(s) by elaborating on how it/they can be achieved. Guidance on how to organize and present the information should also be included here. A checklist can be provided that highlights important points and concepts that students need to understand in order to complete each task. Also include any suggestions and advice on how to structure and organize the material for what will be the ultimate result of the project, and how you would like students to present the material, such as summary tables and graphs.

Resources

All of the resources required for completing the WebQuest need to be provided to students from the outset, and can either be incorporated in the 'Process' section or included in their own section. Resources include all webpage links, and any additional media (including audio, video, and textbooks) that students will be expected to access in order to complete their assigned task(s). Ideally, each resource item when listed should also contain a brief annotation so that students know what the link or resource is referring to and how it can assist them in completing the task.

Evaluation

A rubric to assess students in their completion of the task, and their understanding of the content worked through, needs to be developed. Students should be presented with the rubric so they have an understanding of what is expected of them, and how they will be assessed.

Conclusion

In the final section of the WebQuest, students need to present or submit the results of their task(s) for assessment. In this section also, the teacher needs to provide students with reflection on the topic either by using rhetorical questions or by asking discussion-based questions that help transfer the knowledge gained through completion of the WebQuest to a broader context, as well as into other aspects of the local teaching and learning environment.

11

How would I use a tool to create a WebQuest?

Once designed and set up, a WebQuest is essentially a worksheet or a web page laid out in a particular format. However, it is much more than just a 'lesson planning form' to be filled in; it is a self-contained learning unit that students can follow, explore, and complete. A WebQuest can therefore be developed as a web page in a learning management system (LMS) like Edmodo, Moodle, or Schoology. Alternatively, a WebQuest could be posted to a social networking site under a group that students could join. The WebQuest could also be run from a hard drive with all files saved locally. In any of these cases, all that is required is that the media, and any follow-up links intended for use in the process section, are posted and are readily accessible by students.

Websites that allow the hosting and authoring of WebQuests by teachers are also available. QuestGarden and Zunal are two, and both offer the online authoring of a WebQuest, and the hosting of it so that other teachers can search and use the learning material as well. However, while WebQuests are available on a number of topics from these websites, any content developed by other teachers should be assessed for suitability with your own classes, teaching style, and students, and modified accordingly.

While QuestGarden follows the WebQuest model very strictly, Zunal allows for the inclusion of a number of additional resources whiche include adding games, pre- and post-tests, and Google Map-based activities. Both sites are free to start and have a membership or pro account option available as an upgrade. QuestGarden and Zunal are similar to each other and have their own advantages as a WebQuest hosting or creation service. QuestGarden has been around the longest, while Zunal is a more recent addition to the WebQuest community.

The choice is yours, but please keep in mind that tools and websites do at times change the features that they offer and the layout of the interface. Some may even become defunct.

The following guides have been written in a way that any such changes will not impact on understanding the essential mechanisms behind the use of the WebQuest model, nor on the development of a good WebQuest using any available web-based template.

11A. QuestGarden

Preparation

QuestGarden allows for a 30-day free trial before there is a need to subscribe to a 2-year membership. Any WebQuests created during the trial period will remain active and available after the trial ends, so that they can be downloaded in a zip file for hosting elsewhere if desired. The QuestGarden site allows you to search for, and use, existing WebQuests created by other teachers, and it allows you to use them as-is or to modify them. You can create one of your own as well. The tutorial here will cover the process of creating a WebQuest of your own.

Step One – Getting started

To get started with the QuestGarden website, sign up for a free trial by going to the homepage and clicking on 'Register for a free trial'. The free trial allows for the creation of an unlimited amount of WebQuests, and for them to be downloaded in a zip file if needed (even after the trial period is over). The paid membership feature allows for WebQuest editing and creation past the trial period, and access to a wider range of templates for WebQuest creation. However, once you have signed up, a site profile will need to be created. Your personal information can then be entered, after which you will be taken to the 'Member dashboard'.

Step Two – Exploring the site

After becoming a member, there are several site options to explore. You can 'Learn about WebQuests' by going over the videos hosted on the site by Bernie Dodge – videos discussing good examples, and the common development mistakes made when creating a WebQuest. You can choose to click on 'Collaborate with others' to see who is currently online, and make comments on WebQuest as they are being developed. Otherwise, you may simply want to take some time to search for examples on a specific topic.

Step Three – Search for examples

Prior to the development of a WebQuest, it is a good idea to review others until you are comfortable with the format and the expectations associated with their development. Click 'Search for examples' to begin looking for WebQuests by keyword, or by specific grade and curriculum area. It is also possible to conduct a search based on a WebQuest design pattern (for example, alternate history, persuasive message, travel plan). After you feel comfortable with the type of WebQuests on offer from the site, and have gained enough familiarity with the site after navigating through all of its resources, you may want to start to develop your own WebQuest for the site to host.

Step Four – Creation: Template use

Click 'Create a WebQuest' then 'Click here' to begin editing your first WebQuest for hosting on QuestGarden. A template will then be provided that will walk you through the major sections of creation. These include looking at the 'Goals and context' of the WebQuest (for example, the topic, curriculum standards, and the teaching and learning environment), any associated 'Task and assessment' elements (for example, the problem that students will address), the 'Process' that students will engage in (for example, the how and when of the resources they will use), and any other 'Final details' (for example, an introduction and conclusion, and how the work can be adapted for use by other teachers). Further options include adding 'Polish' to the WebQuest (for example, adjusting the layout and adding images to enhance the presentation for learners), as well as some necessary distribution and hosting 'Tools' (for example, 'Preview', Publish', 'Export', and 'Read comments').

Step Five – Goals and context

In this section of the template, you will need to initially choose a design pattern from the list provided and click 'Select'. After that, you will be presented with an example format that illustrates how each section will guide you. After reviewing this information, click on 'Title/authors/group' to enter these details, information such as a description of your WebQuest, and a record of the grade level and the curriculum area associated with it. Click on 'Standards' to add the standards covered by the WebQuest, and 'Learners' to enter further information about the students intended to undertake the WebQuest. You will then come across 'Checkpoint 1', which can be used to make notes regarding aspects of any part of the materials that need to be improved, and for making general comments about this stage of the lesson. Any comments that are made here will appear in the comments section of the lesson.

Step Six – Task and assessment

In this section of the template, click on 'Introduction' to get started on writing the introduction for the WebQuest, and 'Task' to input elements of the learners' end goal(s), and the focus of their activities. 'Evaluation' will then allow you to edit an existing four-point rubric to suit your own teaching and learning context. This will see you reach 'Checkpoint 2', which allows you to confirm that the task and the evaluations marry up, and that the task is an appropriate one for the WebQuest. As in Checkpoint

1, any comments created under here will also appear in the lesson comments section.

Step Seven – Process

The 'Process' section starts out with a reminder of the importance of finding suitable web-based resources for the learner audience. There is space for three different processes, 'Process 1', 'Process 2', and 'Process 3', and each of these areas allows you to enter the steps involved with each process and the required resources. As with the previous section, all details are entered into the WYSIWYG (what you see is what you get) HTML editor, with the example tabs providing some support for use of the pattern selected. Again, you are able to see a design view, source view, or a preview of the information being edited, and you must click 'Save' in order to store the information before moving on to the next area or section. Once completed, 'Checkpoint 3' will be reached, and again, comments left here will be visible on the lesson comments section of the WebQuest. A number of questions are posed so that checks can be made concerning the learning material developed for this section and the appropriateness of its use with students.

Step Eight – Final Details

The 'Final details' section allows for the development of a 'Conclusion', along with a 'Teacher Intro', 'Teacher resources', 'Teacher process', and 'Credits' areas. The 'Conclusion' needs to focus on elements such as a summary of the goals and details of the WebQuest, and take into account student reflection on their learning. You could also provide links to areas of further study for students as well. The remaining areas are for you to complete with information that can be used by other teachers, so that they can see how your WebQuest can be adaptable or useable in their teaching and learning contexts. Now you come to 'Checkpoint 4' which gives you a chance to review all elements of this section with guided questions, and where, as before, any comments will be visible in the lesson comment area.

Step Nine – Polish and finalization

In the 'Polish' section there is an area available to 'Add images' where there are several links to a number of image resource sites, and a small example of how to use the WYSIWIG editor to add an image to the WebQuest. Clicking 'Appearance' will open up a new browser window or tab so that you can see your WebQuest and make adjustments to the appearance of the titles, headers, navigation bar, body text, and links. 'Checkpoint 5' is the last of the checkpoints, and like all the others before it, provides some guided questions to help you think about how you have developed this section of the WebQuest, and how you can improve upon it if necessary. Your WebQuest is now complete, but there are several site tools that are important to review.

Step Ten – Tools

The 'Tools' section of the template offers 'Preview', 'Publish', 'Export' and 'Read comments' areas. Click on 'Preview' to open a new browser window or tab to see how others will view the completed WebQuest when it is hosted. The 'Publish' section allows you to publish your Webquest, and there are several choices which include keeping either the URL of the WebQuest known to only yourself or making it available to others, and granting permission for your material to be used by other teachers. A tiny URL can also be created here by paid subscribers. The 'Export' option allows you to download a zip file of your WebQuest, and any comments that have been made on the WebQuest can be viewed here (including your own). You can also reply to any comments from this page.

11B. Zunal

Preparation

Zunal is free to register, and offers its service to pre- and in-service teachers as well as faculty to create and share WebQuests with each other. The Zunal site allows you to search for and use existing WebQuests created by other teachers, and it allows you to use them as-is, or to create your own using their online template. By registering with the site, you have a free account which allows you to create just one WebQuest. To create more you need to select an upgrade to a pro-account, which allows you to not only create additional WebQuests, but it allows you to copy and enhance other WebQuests, present ad free WebQuests, and add additional modules to your WebQuests (for example, a quiz, a Google Map-based activity, games like hangman, or additional blank pages). A group account is also possible as a special subscription option. Nonetheless, the tutorial here will cover the process behind the creation of a single WebQuest using the free account type.

Step One – Getting Started

To get started with the Zunal website go to the home page and click 'Register'. After entering your details and registering, you will be taken to the 'My profile' page.

Step Two – Exploring the site

After becoming a member, there are several site options to explore. You can begin by expanding your profile, or changing the information thatyou have entered about yourself (for example, your school, your photo, or your password). You can also upgrade or delete your account from here. This page also allows you to view, delete, or update the WebQuests you have created, see a list of any WebQuests that you have made favorites, and develop your own WebQuest. The menu options along the top of the screen allow you to 'Browse' the WebQuests available by curriculum and grade level, browse a 'Help' question and answer page, or ask 'Questions' about, or provide suggestions for, the Zunal WebQuest Maker. An option to return to the 'My dashboard' is available from the top menu as well.

Step Three – Search the site

Prior to the development of a WebQuest it is a good idea to review others until you are comfortable with the format and the expectations associated with their development. From the top level menu, click on 'Browse', and from this page you will be able to see how many WebQuests are available by grade level and curriculum. You can click to explore the WebQuests available for each, or alternatively you can click on the 'Search' tab to perform a keyword search with or without curriculum and grade level as operators. After you have completed a few searches, reviewed several of the WebQuests available, and feel comfortable with the type of WebQuests on offer, you may want to develop your own WebQuest for the site to host.

Step Four – Creation: Template use

To start creating a WebQuest at Zunal, click on 'Create a WebQuest' from the 'My Dashboard' page, then 'Create a WebQuest from scratch', and enter a title for your WebQuest. (Alternatively, if you are a pro-member, you can copy and enhance a WebQuest).

Step Five – The WebQuest template page

After entering a title for your WebQuest, you will be taken to the WebQuest template page. Along the top, you will be able to see the title of your WebQuest as well as 'Add to favorites' and 'Preview mode'. Along the left side, you will find three areas of buttons, one for developing the WebQuest (from the introduction to the conclusion), one consisting of various tools relating to the WebQuest (for example, statistics and exporting features), and an area for pro-members called 'Add to your WebQuest' (which includes a settings and publishing feature, as well as various additional modules that you can use to add value to your WebQuest like including games, quizzes, and Google Map-based activities). In the center of the screen is a WYSIWIG (What You See Is What You Get) HTML editor where the results of your editing and your WebQuest appear. Directly below that is an 'Add resource button' that will allow you to upload various documents and links, and directly below that again is the public URL of the WebQuest you are going to create.

Step Six – Developing the WebQuest

On entering the WebQuest template page, you will be at the 'Welcome' screen of your WebQuest. It is here where you can update the 'WebQuest Information', which includes adding a description, and some keywords, and identifying the appropriate grade level and curriculum area for its use. If you wish to add a welcoming image, click on 'Update image' to upload one from your computer; click on 'Update WebQuest Information' to change the name, description, grade level, curriculum, keywords, and author; click on 'Add resources' to add a content section, website URLs, local files, local photos, videos from other websites (including YouTube, and TeacherTube), a Voki, or a Glogster poster; and then click on 'Preview Mode' to see how the WebQuest will appear. 'Admin mode' will return you to editing. When you are happy with the welcome screen, you can begin to work on the other elements of the WebQuest.

Step Seven – Introduction

To begin working on the other elements of the WebQuest, click on the appropriate button in the developing WebQuest area (for example, introduction, task, process, evaluation, conclusion, or teacher page). After clicking on 'introduction', you will be able to follow a similar process as that of creating the 'Welcome' page. Information, in the form of 'Help', is provided to guide in the development of the elements for the Introduction. After reading the help provided, click 'Update content', and you will be presented with four sections to complete.

- 'Advice to teachers' – to describe the WebQuest, the amount of time it should take to deliver, and other details for teachers who may want to use or adapt the content with their classes.
- 'Standards' – where you can enter the list of standards that the WebQuest addresses.
- 'Credits' – where you can thank others and provide permission for content or resource usage.
- 'Other' – to add further information if needed.

Once you have completed these sections, click 'Save now' and you will be returned to the 'Introduction' page of the template. You will then be able to 'Update image' or 'Add resources' to the section if you wish, and you can also 'Reset' the page', 'Rename' the page, 'Hide' the page, and move the page 'Up' and 'Down' within the order of presentation.

Step Eight – Task

After completing the 'Introduction' section of the template, click on 'Task' to continue building the WebQuest. Here, you will be provided with some help, in the form of text to guide you in the development of this section (just as in the introduction). When you are ready to enter the appropriate details for the section, click on 'Update content' and you will be taken to a basic WYSIWIG editor. At the bottom of the editor are the definitions of a task, an example, and a rubric to help you in task development. Once you have entered the task elements, previewed them if necessary, and are happy with them, click 'Save now' to record the changes and return to the WebQuest template page. You can then

'Update image' or 'Update resources' for the task if you wish, and continue to the 'Process' section of the WebQuest template.

Step Nine – Process

Click on 'Process' and you will be taken to the process page where you will be guided in text form, as in the previous pages. When ready you can click on 'Update content' to begin adding elements and reviewing them in a similar manner as previous sections. When you have checked the page in 'Preview mode' and you are satisfied, return to 'Admin mode' and 'Update image' or 'Add resources' before moving on to the 'Evaluation' section.

Step Ten – Evaluation

Click on 'Evaluation' to begin editing this section using the template. Once again, you will be provided with help in the form of text, and the means to edit the section in the same manner as previous sections. There is also the ability to edit a provided rubric template, but you will need to change the 'Ratings', the 'Category of assessment' and the factors that align the categories to the ratings, and a possible 'score'. Obviously, you may upload a link, a file, or an image of your own rubric if you choos and you would need to click 'Hide rubric' so that the provided template rubric is not shown. After you have previewed the page, you can move on to the next section of the template.

Step Eleven – Conclusion and teacher page

Click on 'Conclusion' to begin editing the final section of the WebQuest for students. As in previous sections, you will be provided with help in the form of text, and the means to edit the section in the way described previously. After returning to the WebQuest template, the 'Teacher page' is the next option to click after conclusion where the details for this section can be (and should have been already) entered from the 'Welcome' page. If not, or if changes need to be applied, then you can do these now by clicking on the 'Teacher page', and then editing the section in a similar fashion as all of those previous. Congratulations! The WebQuest, and notes for any other teacher who may wish to use it, is now complete and ready for use with students.

Step Twelve – Tools of the WebQuest

Of course, having a ready WebQuest would not be complete without being able to at least share or review it, and this is where the tools of the WebQuest section are important. This section consists of 'About the author(s)', 'Evaluate the WebQuest', 'Reviews', 'Statistics', 'Export the Webquest', and 'Share this WebQuest'. Click 'About the author(s)' and then 'Update profile information' or add another author if you want to share development of the WebQuest. Click on 'Evaluate WebQuest' to provide a self-evaluation of the WebQuest using a pre-fabricated rubric. The rubric is lengthy and very detailed, so it might be wise to click 'Print rubric' to go over a hard copy if required. Click on 'Reviews' to see the number of reviews, approved reviews, and reviews awaiting approval. You can also click on 'Write a review' to provide a star rating (from 1 to 5) to accompany it. Click 'Statistics' to see details of the level of completion for each section of the WebQuest in terms of percent. Click 'Export WebQuest' to export the WebQuest in one of three formats: Adobe PDF, Microsoft Word, or Microsoft Excel. Finally, click 'Share this WebQuest' to distribute the WebQuest via email, over Facebook, on Twitter, or on Digg.

12

What are the key points behind WebQuest use in the TESOL context?

Working with WebQuests, particularly those developed for use with second-language learners of English, sees several important key points emerge:

- WebQuests need to be used as inquiry-oriented learning tools.
- WebQuests are extremely teacher-directed and planned; yet they are intensely student-centered.
- WebQuests, depending on their length, have very different learning goals, and exist as short and long-term types.
- WebQuests need to be developed in ways that seek to engage, motiveate, and go beyond rote thinking for learners.
- WebQuests expose learners to authentic material, develop their collaboration skills, and enhance their communicative opportunities and abilities.
- WebQuests follow a well-established format.

- WebQuests are most suited to tasks involving creativity and problems with several possible solutions.
- WebQuest websites can be relied upon as go to authoring tools and depositiories for the creation and housing of WebQuest content.
- WebQuest content can be saved offline, and can be provided to students as an offline activity in environments where continued access to the internet is problematic.

At the end of the day, WebQuests, although developed in the very early days of the internet, have proven themselves to still be relevant to teaching and learning, and they remain adaptable to student needs as well as the curriculum. WebQuests also allow for the teacher to create material that focuses on student development in engaging and motivating ways that can, in turn, inspire collaboration, creativity, and language development.

13

Lesson plan guides, and example implementation

Provided here are lesson plan guides, as well as a fully developed example WebQuest. The guides are meant to assist in the understanding of how to develop a detailed lesson plan, and to describe what each component and stage of a lesson can cover. In addition, the WebQuest example illustrates how a teacher may develop a WebQuest to cover literacy skills (for example, digital literacy and media literacy) alongside the development of reading and writing skills at the end of a unit covering a novel. The included WebQuest is meant for upper intermediate to advanced learners of English as an additional language, and it can be adapted for use with younger learners or those at a lower level. The example classroom content and its handouts may be used as-is, or adapted for use by any teacher.

The content covered here includes:

- Lesson plan general guide
- Lesson plan guide for WebQuest integration
- Example Implementation: WebQuest – Book trailers
- Example Implementation: WebQuest – Book trailers: Handouts

Lesson Plan General Guide	
Teaching Context	
Level of Proficiency and Maturity	Student language level (e.g. beginner, intermediate, advanced). Student age range (e.g. young learners, adults).
Lesson Length	Time allotted for the class (e.g. 35-45 minutes).
Lesson Topic	Major theme or focus of the lesson (e.g. numbers and time).
Objectives	Lesson aims (e.g. to teach students how to tell the time and date accurately).
Outcomes	Learning outcomes (e.g. students will be able to read analog and digital timepieces).
Relevant Prior Learning	Anything that students need to know before starting work on this lesson's content (e.g. students need to have completed Chapter Two of the book, and have previously met language associated with appointments, calendars, and timekeeping).

Teacher Preparation	
Hardware	Types of computer or peripherals required (e.g. USB sticks, MP3 players).
Software	Name of software used (e.g. Photo Story 3, Microsoft Word).
Webpage Links	Hyperlink to web resources (e.g. www.google.com).
Additional Resources	Other necessary materials for the lesson (e.g. handouts, worksheets, textbooks).

Procedure			
Stage and Timing	Objective	Teacher	Students
Review Stage (if required, 5 minutes)	Focus of stage (e.g. encourage the use of previously acquired language).	Indicate what the teacher says and does in each stage of the lesson.	Provide expected examples of student behavior.

Warm-up Stage/Pre-Technology Use (10 minutes)	Focus of stage (e.g. introduce new concepts and language to students in a meaningful manner).	Indicate what the teacher says and does in each stage of the lesson.	Provide expected examples of student behavior.
Main Stage/ Technology-based Activity (20 minutes)	Focus of stage (e.g. allow students to utilize technology to become familiar with and apply the concepts and language content introduced in the lesson).	Indicate what the teacher says and does in each stage of the lesson.	Provide expected examples of student behavior.

Practice Stage (15 minutes)	Focus of stage (e.g. allow learners to utilize the skills and language that they are expected to acquire during the lesson in a practical way).	Indicate what the teacher says and does in each stage of the lesson.	Provide expected examples of student behavior.
Lesson Summation Stage/Post-Technology Activities (10 minutes)	Focus of stage (e.g. instructor reinforces the importance of language concepts and skills acquired, stating how they will be useful in forthcoming lessons).	Indicate what the teacher says and does in each stage of the lesson.	Provide expected examples of student behavior.

Further Considerations	
Follow-Up Activities	Prepare material that can be applied in a follow up class. Also, be ready with activities for students who complete their class work earlier than expected.
Contingency Plan(s)	Always prepare an alternate teaching scenario in case of any problems. For example, a sudden power outage or a timetabling issue could make the assigned room unavailable.
Evaluation	Reflect on what worked well, and what did not, and how you might deliver the lesson differently or improve upon it when running it again.

Lesson Plan Guide for WebQuest Integration	
Teaching Context	
Level of Proficiency and Maturity	Upper Intermediate to advanced. Can be modified for younger learners or lower language levels.
Lesson Length	Five lessons (over a week). Homework completion components. Time allotted for each class: 50 minutes.
Lesson Topic	Variable, from integration with a novel through to a unit on entertainment or on movie reviews to other forms of presentation.
Objectives	1. Develop critical thinking skills. 2. Enhance communication skills by asking questions, expressing opinions, developing narratives, and writing for an audience. 3. Strengthen media literacy and digital literacy skills (use software, images, audio, video, and other media elements or components). 4. Advance reading and writing skills. 5. Develop presentation and pitching abilities.

Outcomes	1. Students will complete a WebQuest on book trailers (refer to the 'WebQuest example: Book trailers'). 2. Students will employ a range of media to complete their WebQuest task. 3. Students will show evidence of critical thinking, the ability to effectively evaluate and critique content, and use rubrics effectively.
Relevant Prior Learning	Students will need to be familiar with digital storytelling in order to develop a book trailer, and have read the associated novel in the target or first language.

Teacher Preparation	
Hardware	Computer or tablet, with internet access and microphone, camera, and scanner (if scanning student work) for each group. USB sticks, YouTube, or Google Drive for storage of the developed book trailer.
Software	Media player. Digital storytelling tools (Photo Story 3, iMovie, or WeVideo). Note-taking tools (Microsoft Word or Pages – as required).
Webpage Links	See the resources section of the 'WebQuest example: Book trailers'.
Additional Resources	See the handout section of the 'WebQuest example: Book trailers'.

Procedure – Day 1 of 5			
Stage and Timing	Objective	Teacher	Students
Review Stage (5 minutes)	Remind students of a novel that they have read for class or for leisure. Ask about what made it exciting and interesting for them. Start to introduce aspects of language that students can use when creating a book trailer for the novel.	Teacher directs questions to have students start brainstorming on a recent novel that they have read for class or for leisure.	Students briefly tell about their pet or their weekend in story format, using appropriate sequencers.
Warm-up Stage/Pre-Technology Use (15 minutes)	Introduce the WebQuest and book trailer concept.	Provide students with the WebQuest worksheets.	Students go through the WebQuest sections with the teacher.

Main Stage (20 minutes)	The WebQuest has been introduced and students will complete Steps one and two by the end of class.	The teacher guides students in the completion of Steps one and two of the WebQuest.	Students complete Steps one and two of the WebQuest along with the associated handouts.
Lesson Summation Stage/Post-Technology Activities (10 minutes)	Students should be reminded of the lesson's goals. Each of the objectives of Step one and of Step two of the WebQuest should have been completed.	Ensure students have completed Handouts one, two, and three. Provide feedback and advice on how the handouts have been completed.	Students should have completed Handouts one, two, and three by this stage of the lesson. These can be completed for homework if work is still required on them.

Procedure – Day 2 of 5			
Stage and Timing	**Objective**	**Teacher**	**Students**
Review Stage (5 minutes)	Remind students of the WebQuest goals and tasks. Ensure that all students have completed Steps one and two along with the associated handouts.	Ensure students are up to date with the task, and are ready to begin Step three.	Students should have completed all tasks, and they are ready to start Step three of the WebQuest.
Warm-up Stage/Pre-Technology Use (5 minutes)	Go through the steps required to complete a book trailer under step three of the WebQuest.	Ensure students understand the steps they need to perform by the end of class.	Students should be provided with the necessary handouts, and access to the technology required.

Main Stage (35 minutes)	Students use the handouts to brainstorm their script, develop their storyboard, collect media for book trailer development, and begin to produce their trailer.	Assist students in working on the development of their book trailer, and ensure that they are working through the resources and handouts effectively.	Students begin to work through Handout four, five, six, and seven to complete their book trailer and the required minimum production requirements.
Lesson Summation Stage/Post-Technology Activities (5 minutes)	Students should have been able to complete the storyboard for their trailer, and be at the media collection or trailer finalization stage of Step three.	Ensure students have started to successfully develop their trailer using the applications that they have chosen.	Students should have completed Handouts four, five, and six at a minimum.

Procedure – Day 3 of 5			
Stage and Timing	**Objective**	**Teacher**	**Students**
Review Stage (5 minutes)	Remind students that they will need to complete Step three of the WebQuest by the end of this lesson.	Ensure that students have completed Handouts four, five and six.	Students are able to produce their completed handouts.
Warm-up Stage/Pre-Technology Use (5 minutes)	Remind students of the storyboarding process and the requirements that need to be met.	Ensure students understand how to use the application to complete their trailer, and are familiar with the checklist requirements from Handout seven.	Students should prepare their media and get ready to use the application that they have chosen to create their book trailer.

Main Stage (35 minutes)	Students should be working on finalizing their book trailer according to the required checklist.	Assist students where necessary as they complete their book trailer.	Students will use their storyboard and collected media to finalize their book trailer.
Lesson Summation Stage/Post-Technology Activities (5 minutes)	Students should have been able to develop their book trailer in full.	Ensure that students have successfully developed their trailer, and have completed the final checklist of Step three, using handout seven.	Students will need to complete Step three of the WebQuest by this stage of the lesson. Otherwise, completion will need to be set as a homework task.

Procedure – Day 4 of 5			
Stage and Timing	**Objective**	**Teacher**	**Students**
Review Stage (5 minutes)	Students should have completed their book trailer, and be able to now start work on their presentation and pitch regarding it.	The teacher ensures that all trailers have been completed, and that students have them ready for playback to the class.	Students will need to download their book trailer to the class computer or have it ready to playback from an online source.
Warm-up Stage/Pre-Technology Use (5 minutes)	Introduce Steps four, five, and six of the WebQuest to students.	Guide students in completing work on their pitch to present their book trailer.	Students will need to use Handout eight to help them prepare their pitch.

Main Stage (25 minutes)	Students work together to prepare a short pitch to accompany the playback of their book trailer.	Assist students in completing their pitch. It should be concise, and they should aim to speak one sentence each.	Students successfully sequence their story, and record an appropriate narrative with teacher guidance.
Lesson Summation Stage/Post-Technology Activities (10 minutes)	Students should be ready to play back their book trailer, and present their pitch in the following class.	Ensure that students have completed their pitch and are ready to present it in the following class.	Students will be able to review their pitch, and practice it for homework before presenting it in class the following day.

Procedure – Day 5 of 5			
Stage and Time	Objective	Teacher	Students
Review Stage **(5 minutes)**	Review the WebQuest components so far completed, and introduce the steps to be completed for the lesson.	Ensure that students understand the steps needed to be completed for the day, and distribute the necessary handouts.	Students prepare to evaluate and critique others work, as well as present and pitch their book trailer to the class.
Warm-up Stage/Pre-Technology Use **(5 minutes)**	Student groups are given a short-time to practice their pitch and prepare their book trailer for playback.	Ensure students are ready to present, and are ready to evaluate others using handout nine.	Students have their note cards ready and are reviewing for their pitch.

Main Stage (35 minutes)	Students play back their book trailer, pitch their presentation, evaluate other trailers, and write a critique on each.	Guide students to present and play back their trailer, and keep to the set time limit.	Students will use Handout nine to evaluate each book trailer, and Handout ten to critique each book trailer.
Lesson Summation Stage/Post-Technology Activities (5 minutes)	A class response system, like Plickers, should be used to take a vote for the best produced book trailer.	Distribute and scan Plicker cards, and reveal the vote to the class.	Students hold up their Plicker card to vote for the trailer that they believe to be the best.

Further Considerations	
Follow-Up Activities	The book trailers can be included in student portfolios for end of semester or end of term assessment. The book trailers can be used to inspire future students who take this class to read the novel.
Contingency Plan(s)	Several activity sheets for review of previous material should be prepared to allow those students who complete tasks to keep busy with language content. Alternatively, some off-line language games can be prepared to fill in the time if technological problems occur.
Evaluation	What are the biggest frustrations for implementation? Can these be remedied next time? What are the successes of the lesson? What did students get out of this activity? Can more language practice be provided?

WebQuest Example – Book Trailers

Introduction

The world of book publishing can be an exciting place, and this is where you and your team work – in the offices of one of the world's most famous book publishers. There is an upcoming book launch, and your boss needs an award winning book trailer.

Task

There is a book launch scheduled for next month, and the author needs a book trailer specifically developed for their book. You will work in a team to prepare a book trailer for the author.

You will need to:

- Review several successful book trailers
- Learn how to create a successful book trailer
- Present and pitch your book trailer
- Evaluate and critique other book trailers
- Vote on the best book trailer to represent the book on launch day

Process

Step one – What is a book trailer?

Review existing book trailers:

1. Watch at least five different book trailers
2. List five things that you think make for a good book trailer
3. List five things that you think make for a bad book trailer

Step two – Creating a book trailer

Understand the process behind making a book trailer:

1. Identify the stages behind creating a book trailer
2. Select software to create a book trailer

Step three – Producing a book trailer

Create a unique book trailer by working through:

1. Brainstorming
2. Storyboarding
3. Script development
4. Media collection
5. Trailer finalization
6. A checklist

Step Four – Presenting a book trailer

In this step you will need to present and pitch your book trailer:

1. Play it – share your book trailer
2. Pitch it – 'sell' your book trailer

Step five – Evaluating and critiquing

In this step you will need to evaluate and critique peer' book trailers:

1. Evaluate – peers' book trailers
2. Write up – the good and the bad

Step six – Vote

In this step you will need to vote for the best trailer using a classroom response system:

1. Plickers – vote for the best book trailer

Resources

Step one

In this step you will use several web resources, and an in-class handout to view several book trailers, identify what makes a book trailer good or bad, and prepare a list of the good and bad aspects of a book trailer.

1. Go to Book Trailers for Readers (http://www.booktrailersforreaders.com/), and watch at least five different book trailers.

2. Then think about what makes the good trailers good and the bad trailers bad. How did they captivate you? Did the trailers make you really want to read those books? Think about these kinds of questions while you review the following web sites:

   a) Fantastic book trailers and the reasons why they're good (Najafi, 2013)

   b) Why most book trailers are awful and how yours can be different (Goins, 2016)

   c) Book trailers and using video for book marketing (Penn, 2015)

   d) What makes a good book trailer (JLG, 2016)

3. Finally, list five things that make for a good book trailer, and five things that make for a bad book trailer.

    a) Handout one – 'Book trailers: The good and the bad'

Step two

In this step, you will identify the various stages behind creating a book trailer, identify appropriate software to help you create a book trailer, and detail these aspects on the in-class handout.

1. Identify the stages behind a book trailer

    a) Book trailers for readers (Harclerode, n.d.)

    b) How to make a book trailer: 6 tips (Sambuchino, 2016)

    c) How to make a book trailer for free (that looks professional) (Natsil, 2015)

    d) 12 easy steps to the making of a book trailer (Croome, 2011)

2. Identify the software available to create a book trailer

    a) Spotlight on business: 4 elements of an awesome animoto book trailer (Schiller, 2015)

    b) Book trailers: 11 Steps to make your own (Penn, 2008)

3. Detail the steps that your group will follow when creating a book trailer, along with the applications available and what makes these good choices to use when producing a book trailer. Finally, decide upon an application that your group will use to produce a book trailer.

    a) Handout two – 'Book trailers: Steps to create a book trailer'

    b) Handout three – 'Book trailers: Applications to use'

Step three

Now you will produce your book trailer. You need to take into account script development, storyboarding, media collection, and trailer finalization before conducting a checklist to ensure that you have met the production criteria as set by your teacher.

1. *Brainstorming*

    Prior to starting out, start thinking about the book. Who are the main characters in the book? How do you feel when you think about them? What is the mood of the book? How does this mood make you feel? What images come to mind when you feel this way? What is the plot of the book? What captured you about the plot the most? Why would someone want to read this book? How would you persuade them to read the book? How would you interest them in the book? What images or video could you use to engage or connect them to the book? What details from the book did you find to be the most exciting, interesting, and funny? What other details could make someone want to read the book?

    a) Handout four – 'Book trailers: brainstorming'

2. *Script development*

    You will need to develop a short narration for your book trailer, as well as think about any on-screen captions that you may want to use. You can use the blurb of the book to help you prepare a summary. Try to use vocabulary that will persuade the viewer to read the book, engage them in the story, and keep them interested until the end. Start by thinking of an interesting 'hook' or captivating question based on a plot point to draw in the viewer. Use the appropriate handout to write out your summary and any desired on-screen captions.

    a) Handout five – 'Book trailers: Summary'

3. *Storyboard*

    The summary that you use for narration, along with any captions that you want to include in your trailer, will need to match any images, music, or video clips that you may also want to use for your book trailer. You also need to see how long your book trailer will be, based on the recording of your summary and how long you think each image, music clip, or video clip will play for.

   a) Handout six – 'Book trailers: Storyboard'

4. *Media collection*

   You will need to find images, music clips, video clips, and other media to use in the development of your book trailer. Pay attention to copyright, and only use images, music clips, or video clips that are in the public domain or are usable when crediting the creator.

   a) Images: Pics4Learning (Tech4Learning, 2016)

   b) Music: Free music archive (FMA, 2016)

   c) Video: Mazwai (Mazwai, 2016)

5. *Trailer finalization*

   Use the application that you selected to produce and finalize your book trailer. Reviewing a tutorial on how to use the application to make a book trailer can help you get started and get finished much more quickly.

    a) Book trailer tutorial using (Windows) Movie Maker (Lion, 2014)

    b) How to create an Animoto book trailer (Doyle, 2015)

6. *Checklist*

Ensure that your group has met the minimum production, language use, and playback requirements as set by your teacher.

    a) Handout Seven – 'Book trailers: Trailer finalization checklist'

Step four

This is where you will need to present your book trailer to the class, and it involves playing the book trailer, and then speaking about it. You need to pitch the trailer as being the best to represent the book on launch, and each group member must give at least one reason for this trailer to be chosen as the best.

1. Play it.
   a) Upload your video to a site such as YouTube for online sharing and playback, or
   b) Upload your video to a USB drive to play back locally
2. Pitch it.
   a) How to do a presentation in class (WikiHow, 2016)
   b) Handout eight – 'Book trailers: Pitch it!'

Step five

In this step, you need to evaluate and critique the book trailers produced by each class group. You should do this in two ways.

1. Use the rubric to help you think about the book trailers as you watch them, then complete the associated handout after each book trailer has completed playing.
   a) Handout nine – 'Book trailers: Book trailer evaluation rubric'

2. After watching all of the other groups' trailers and listening to their presentations, write one paragraphs identifying at least one good and one bad aspect of each trailer, and submit these to your teacher for review.

   a) Handout ten – 'Book trailers: Critique'

3. At the same time that you are doing all of this your teacher will evaluate your book trailer.

   a) Handout nine – 'Book trailers: Book trailer evaluation rubric'

Step six

Here, you will watch each trailer again, one by one, and then vote for the one that you think is the best. A classroom response system will be used by the teacher to gather the votes anonymously.

1. Playback.

   a) YouTube or USB

2. Voting.

   a) Plickers classroom response system (Plickers, 2016)

Evaluation

Any book can be used for this WebQuest. However, it would be best if it is a novel that students have been studying recently or, perhaps for older students, a popular movie that is based on a book.

1. The completed book trailer can be evaluated using:
   a) Handout nine – 'Book trailers: Book trailer evaluation rubric'.
2. The completed WebQuest can be evaluated using:
   a) Handout eleven – 'Book trailers: WebQuest evaluation rubric'.

Conclusion

Students

1. Each group of students completes and presents a book trailer to the class as a group, and pitches why it is the best one for the author to use for their book.
2. Students write a one-paragraph critique of each book trailer, including their own, and are able to identify what makes for good and bad

book trailers. The paragraph is submitted as a writing sample for the teacher to review.

3. Students use a rubric to identify the best class-produced book trailer, and the one that they think would be best used to sell the book.

Teacher

1. The teacher closes the WebQuest with a summary of the topic and the goals achieved by the students throughout its completion.

2. The best book trailer, as voted by the class, is identified.

3. The entire WebQuest is assessed the teacher

    a) Handout eleven: 'Book trailers – WebQuest evaluation rubric'

WebQuest example – Book Trailers: Handouts

1. The good and the bad
2. Steps to create a book trailer
3. Applications to use
4. Brainstorming
5. Summary
6. Storyboarding
7. Trailer finalization checklist
8. Pitch it!
9. Book trailer evaluation rubric
10. Critique
11. WebQuest evaluation rubric

1. Book Trailers: The Good and the Bad

Group Members

Good book trailers ...

1. _____
   _____
2. _____
   _____
3. _____
   _____
4. _____
   _____
5. _____
   _____

Bad book trailers ...

1. _____
   _____
2. _____
   _____
3. _____
   _____
4. _____
   _____
5. _____
   _____

2. Book Trailers: Steps to Create a Book Trailer

Group Members

Steps to Create a Book Trailer

Step 1. _____
Description _____
_____

Step 2. _____
Description _____
_____

Step 3. _____
Description _____
_____

Step 4. _____
Description _____
_____

Step 5. _____
Description _____
_____

(Add more steps if you need them).

3. Book Trailers: Applications to Use

Group Members

Applications to use to create a book trailer

Application 1. _____

_____

Reasons for choosing this application _____

_____

_____

_____

Application 2. _____

_____

Reasons for choosing this application _____

_____

_____

_____

Application 3. _____

_____

Reasons for choosing this application _____

_____

_____

_____

4. Book Trailers: Brainstorming

Group Members

The Book

Title _____

_____

Characters _____

_____

Genre/Mood _____

What is the book about?

Plot Points _____

_____

Hook _____

_____

Why would someone want to read the book?

Persuade _____

Interest _____

Engage _____

Other details from the book

Exciting _____

Interesting _____

Funny _____

Other _____

5. Book Trailers: Summary

Group Members

You will need to develop a short narration for your book trailer, as well as think about any on-screen captions that you may want to use. You can use the blurb of the book to help you prepare a summary of at least five sentences.

Summary _____

_____

_____

_____

_____

_____

_____

_____

_____

_____

_____

On-screen captions _____

_____

_____

_____

_____

6. Book Trailers: Storyboarding

Group Members

Scene Number _____

Image or Video	**Music** _____
	_____
	_____

On-screen caption _____

_____

Summary sentence _____

_____

_____

Scene Number _____

Image or Video	**Music** _____
	_____
	_____

On-screen caption _____

_____

Summary sentence _____

_____

_____

7. Book Trailers: Trailer Finalization Checklist

Group Members

Minimum requirements have been met, and at least:	
Production	☐ Five images have been used
	☐ One video has been used
	☐ One song has been used
Language Use	☐ A five-sentence summary was developed
	☐ One sentence is spoken by each group member
Playback	☐ A trailer has been uploaded to YouTube, or it has been saved to a USB drive
	☐ The trailer has been tested in the classroom for playback

8. Book Trailers: Pitch it!

Group Members

Use notes and keywords as prompts on your cards for your presentation, so that you can recall the information and keep looking at the audience instead of just reading from a piece of paper. Remember that your aim is to sell your book trailer as being the best. Try to use vocabulary to persuade, engage, and keep your audience interested.

Card 1. _____

Card 2. _____

Card 3. _____

Card 4. _____

Card 5. _____

Card 6. _____

Card 7. _____

Card 8. _____

9. Book Trailers: Book Trailer Evaluation Rubric

Group Members

Plot Hook	A captivating question is used, and the plot is not fully exposed.	1 2 3 4 5
Summary	The summary is concise and does not overwhelm the trailer; on-screen captions are not overused.	1 2 3 4 5
Language	Appropriate vocabulary is applied to help persuade, engage, and keep the audience interested.	1 2 3 4 5
Images	Any images used relate well to the narration, and are representative of the plot.	1 2 3 4 5
Music	The genre of music chosen is reflective of the book.	1 2 3 4 5
Video	Any video used relates well to the narration, is representative of the plot, and works well with the accompanying soundtrack.	1 2 3 4 5
Production	The length is appropriate (under 90 seconds), the voice is not overpowered by music, and the video has a logical progression.	1 2 3 4 5
Copyright	Material used is copyright-free or cited appropriately.	1 2 3 4 5
	TOTAL	**/40**

Ratings: 1 Poor 2 Fair 3 Average 4 Good 5 Excellent

10. Book Trailers: Critique

Group Members

Write one paragraph identifying at least one good and one bad aspect of the book trailers that your classmates have prepared.

Paragraph 1. _____

_____

_____

_____

Paragraph 2. _____

_____

_____

_____

Paragraph 3. _____

_____

_____

_____

Paragraph 4. _____

_____

_____

_____

11. Book Trailers: WebQuest Evaluation Rubric

Group Members

Introduction	Goal of WebQuest achieved.	1 2 3 4 5
Task	All tasks completed, and well executed.	
	☐ Reviewed five trailers	1 2 3 4 5
	☐ Created a successful trailer	1 2 3 4 5
	☐ Presented/pitched a trailer	1 2 3 4 5
	☐ Evaluated/critiqued others	1 2 3 4 5
	☐ Voted on the best trailer	1 2 3 4 5
Process	Students worked well as a team, and the final product is a result of equal collaboration.	1 2 3 4 5
Resources	Ideas expressed are based on all the resources provided, but demonstrated originality.	1 2 3 4 5
Evaluation and Conclusion	Students were able to achieve the final Webquest goals.	
	☐ Presented as a group, and pitched successfully	1 2 3 4 5
	☐ One-paragraph critique of others trailers written	1 2 3 4 5
	☐ Rubric used to identify the best trailer; vote submitted	1 2 3 4 5
	TOTAL	**/ 55**

Ratings: 1 Poor 2 Fair 3 Average 4 Good 5 Excellent

14
Photocopiable material

This section contains photocopiable content, and you are free to make as many copies as you require for teaching purposes and preparing your classes. Any other use or distribution should include a citation to the source of the content. In developing your WebQuests, it will prove useful to use the provided worksheet and resource notes as a guide.

The lesson plan template can be used for considering how best to integrate the steps for using the WebQuest with your classes. As such, the template is meant to act as means to begin thinking about how to implement, with your classes, aspects of what has been discovered through this book. The template should be supplemented with any necessary material, along with the staging as well as other aspects of the lesson being adjusted as required.

The following material is available:

- WebQuest worksheet resource notes
- WebQuest worksheet
- Lesson plan template

WebQuest Worksheet Resource Notes	
Title	Choose a title for the WebQuest, and write it here.
Introduction/ Description	Provide an overview and set up any role-playing scenario (e.g. 'You are a linguist investigating the pronunciation of Standard American English').
Task	Describe the end product of activities here. Include details of questions to be answered; details to be analysed, summarized, or organized; positions adopted or to be defended; and so on.
Process	List a step-by-step process for students to follow when completing the task(s).
Resources	Include all required resources and website links, annotated with a brief description.
Evaluation	Develop or utilise a prefabricated rubric to assess students.
Conclusion	Summarize what learners need to accomplish by the end of the WebQuest. Include questions to assist in transferring the knowledge gained to a broader context.

WebQuest Worksheet

Title	
Introduction/ Description	
Task	
Process	
Resources	
Evaluation	
Conclusion	

Lesson Plan Template	
Teaching Context	
Level of Proficiency and Maturity	
Lesson Length	
Lesson Topic	
Objectives	
Outcomes	
Relevant Prior Learning	
Teacher Preparation	
Hardware	
Software	
Webpage Links	
Additional Resources	

Procedure			
Stage and Timing	Objective	Teacher	Students
Review Stage (if required)			
Warm-up Stage/Pre-Technology Use			
Main Stage/ Technology-based Activity			
Practice Stage			
Lesson Summation Stage/Post-Technology Activities			

Further Considerations	
Follow-Up Activities	
Contingency Plan(s)	
Evaluation	

15

Resources list

As sites continuously go down, merge, and emerge, perhaps only a small selection of all appropriate resource content should be presented here. An attempt at keeping the number of resources to a select few for each type also provides a sample that is both comprehensive and extensive, but not overwhelming. Like any other instructor resource list, individuals will be able to add to the content as they find material that is useful, creating their own bookmark list, and over time, come to curate a vast resource library tailored to their individual teaching and learning context. Each section of this list is broken down into applications that are mostly all freely available for use with Android or iOS devices, computers, or web-based platforms.

Teachers who wish to make notes, or to record any additional resources that they come across, can use the notes section at the end of this chapter.

The following content is covered:

- App creation
- Audio creation/editing
- Blogs
- Bookmarking
- Books
- Coding
- Comic strip generators
- Copyright
- Digital story creation
- Image resources
- Image editing
- Interactive whiteboards
- Mashups
- Media timelines
- Music resources
- Podcasting
- Podcatchers
- Presentations
- Publishing
- QR codes
- Rubrics
- Screencasting
- Storyboarding and scripting
- Story creation apps
- Video editing
- Video resources
- WebQuests
- Wikis

App Creation

Android – n/a

iOS – n/a

Computer – n/a

Web

Android Creator [free/paid] creates free Android apps without the need for programming knowledge.

AppMakr [free/paid] is a template based application creator that relies on drag and drop of elements for the development of no-coding required applications. It is available in a variety of languages.

Appy Pie [free/paid] relies on templates as well as drag and drop for users to begin creating their app. It requires no coding skills.

AppYourself [paid] is an app creation tool aimed at the business market.

Como DIY [paid] is a do-it-yourself app creation tool aimed to mostly target to businesses, and is available in a number of languages.

iBuildApp [paid] is a template driven app creator for iPhone and Android phones.

Audio Creation/Editing

Android

PCM Recorder [free] is a simple voice recorder.

Pocket WavePad [free] records edits and adds effects to audio.

TapeMachine [paid] is a graphical sound recorder and editor.

iOS

Pocket WavePad [free] records edits and adds effects to audio.

Voice Memos [paid] is voice recorder that allows multitasking.

Computer

Audacity [free] is an open source digital editing program available for Mac and PC which you can use to record, edit and mix narration and music.

Pocket WavePad [free] records, edits, and adds effects to audio for Mac.

GoldWave [free/paid] is a digital audio editor that provides simple recording as well as more sophisticated processing, restoration, enhancement, and conversion for Windows and Linux. A free version is available for evaluation purposes, after which a lifetime license can be purchased.

Web

Twistedwave [free] is a browser-based audio editor that can record or edit any audio file.

Blogs

Android

Blogaway [free] is a simple application to allow blogging on-the-go. It works with Blogger and allows for post creation, adding of photos, videos, multiple account management, saving of drafts, bookmarking, and a host of formatting options.

iOS

Disqus [free] is a commenting system that can be included in blogs as an add-on. The application provides an easy way to moderate comments and publish responses to keep engagement levels high.

TravelPod – Travel Blog [free] is a blogging application that works on- and offline, and is designed to be used while traveling.

Computer – n/a

Web

Blogger.com [free] will host your blog for free, and aside from being very easy to use, it allows some level of privacy so it can be suitable for use as a class blogging site. From a single account, you can create as many blogs as you wish and determine who is allowed to comment on the content.

BuzzSumo [paid] allows users to search for blog posts that have been highly shared across social media.

Edublogs.org [free] allows teachers to create and mange their own and students' websites. There is room for customization of design and the ability to add various media to this private and secure platform.

Kidblog.org [free] is an easy-to-use, safe, and secure publishing platform designed for students in grades K-12. There are a number of excellent features including privacy and password protection, and there is no need for student personal information to be collected, nor is there any advertising. It is free for up to fifty students per class.

WordPress.org [free] is one of the most popular blogging platforms in use today as it is open-source and is easily customizable. The downloadable software for self-hosting purposes is much more flexible than that available on the blogging platform.

Twitter [free] deserves a mention here as it is useful for microblogging (posting short frequent updates). It allows users to post and read short 140-character posts called 'tweets'.

Tumblr [free] is a blogging platform open to those over thirteen years of age, with most users using pen names over their real names when blogging. Users can post on their blog, follow others, and search posts. It is unique in that posts are divided into media types: text, photo, quote, link, chat, audio, and video.

Bookmarking

Android

Bookmark [free] is a cross-platform app that allows for the syncing of bookmarks across different browsers and devices.

Delicious [free] provides users with the ability to organize links to content on the internet that they would like to save, the ability to discover links, edit tags and comments, and also to explore content saved by friends.

Facebook Save [free] is a built-in option for saving Facebook news content to read at a later date.

Instapaper [free] provides an offline archiving solution for web pages, and it presents this content to be read in newspaper fashion. Content can be highlighted, and notes can be added while reading.

Pinterest [free] allows users to pin posts (for example, web pages, images, and videos) and organize them around a common theme.

Pocket [free] integrates with a large number of third party applications that allow for the building of bookmarks. Web pages, videos, images, and whatever else can be used offline for bookmarking. Archiving maintains the links but removes the content from offline availability.

iOS

Delicious [free] allows users to save content from the internet (including web pages, blog posts, tweets, pictures, and video), and provides options for searching through others' collections of links.

Facebook Save [free] is a built-in option for saving Facebook news content to read at a later date.

Instapaper [free] provides an offline archiving solution for web pages and presents this content to be read in newspaper fashion. Content can be highlighted, and notes can be added while reading.

Pinterest [free] allows users to pin posts (for example, web pages, images, and videos) and organize them around a common theme.

Pocket [free] integrates with a large number of third party applications that allow for the building of bookmarks. Web pages, videos, images, and whatever else can be used offline for bookmarking. Archiving maintains the links but removes the content from offline availability.

Computer

EdwinSoft's UltimateDemon [paid] is link building software that helps to provide search engine optimization to a website.

Pinterest [free] allows users to pin posts (for example, web pages, images, and videos) and organize them around a common theme.

Pocket [free] integrates with a large number of third party applications that allow for the building of bookmarks. Web pages, videos, images, and whatever else can be used offline for bookmarking. Archiving maintains the links but removes the content from offline availability.

ReadKit [trial/paid] offers an Apple Mac curative and archiving platform for the content found in your other bookmarking applications (like Pocket and Instapaper) and RSS readers, and provides an extra level of organization to this content.

Web

Delicious [free] is a social bookmarking site that allows users to bookmark webpages to the internet instead of locally.

Facebook Save [free] is a built-in option for saving Facebook news content to read at a later date.

Instapaper [free] provides an offline archiving solution for web pages, and it presents this content to be read in newspaper fashion. Content can be highlighted, and notes can be added while reading.

OnlyWire [paid] works with WordPress and offers automatic submission of content to social networking and social bookmarking sites.

Pocket [free] integrates with a large number of third party applications that allow for the building of bookmarks. Web pages, videos, images, and whatever else can be used offline for bookmarking. Archiving maintains the links but removes the content from offline availability.

Books

Android

Wattpad Free Books [free] provides access to free stories and books written by aspiring authors.

iOS

Free Books – Ultimate Classics Library [free] features free access to 23,469 classic books.

Computer – n/a

Web

BookRix [free] allows access to thousands of books to read either online or to download as ebooks.

Children's Storybooks Online [free] provides a series of illustrated stories for all ages to read.

Coding

Android

Run Marco! [free] offers users the opportunity to play an adventure game while they learn to code. The application presents instructions using 'Blocky', which is the same as that used by the official Hour of Code tutorials.

Tynker [free] is an easy way for children to learn programming skills as they solve puzzles to learn concepts and build games, or control robots and drones. A number of templates are available for free.

iOS

Codea [paid] is a software development tool that uses the Lua programming language to teach users how to program.

Hopscotch [free] is an application that allows users to begin learning to code by making games similar to Angry Birds, and sharing them so others can play them.

ScratchJr [free] allows users to program their own interactive stories and games by snapping together graphical programming blocks. The application was inspired by the Scratch programming language.

Tynker [free] is an easy way for children to learn programming skills as they solve puzzles to learn concepts and build games, or control robots and drones. A number of templates are available for free.

Computer

Scratch [free] allows users to create stories, games, and animations using the Scratch programming language, and then share these with others. It is a project of the Lifelong Kindergarten Group at the MIT Media Lab.

Lightbot – Programming Puzzles [paid] is an OS X game-based application that allows players to use programming logic to solve levels. The app is also available for Android and iOS devices.

Web – n/a

Comic Strip Generators

Android

Comic Maker [free] creates comics from the photo gallery.

Comic Strip It! Lite [free] takes photos or use photo gallery images to create a comic.

iOS

Comic Life 3 [paid] turns photos into comic pages, or creates an entire comic from scratch using templates to build pages with speech balloons, comic lettering, and photo filters.

ToonTastic [free] is a wizard-based animated comic or cartoon creator.

Strip Designer [paid] is software for comic creation that uses camera, library, or Facebook photo options to create a comic.

Computer

Comic Creator [paid] is a basic template driven comic creator for use on a Windows computer.

Web

> *Pixton* [free/paid] is an easy to use comprehensive online comic creator that supports narration, and offers a range of signup options from a free fun option to paid educator/business accounts.
>
> *MakeBeliefsComix* [free] is a basic comic creator that uses black and white images over a four-panel comic strip. An iOS version is also available.
>
> *Toonlet* [free] allows for anyone to create their own cartoon characters and web comics.
>
> *Toondoo* [free] allows for the drag and drop creation of comic strips. An iOS version is also available.

Copyright

Android – n/a

iOS – n/a

Computer – n/a

Web

> *Creative Commons Licenses* [free] gives detailed information regarding the various types of licensing afforded to creative commons, and the permissions that each license grants for the use specific works.

> *Image Codr* [free] can assist learners and teachers alike in determining how a Flickr image can be used (as determined by the original photographer), and provides users with an automatically generated Creative Commons citation regarding the images use within digital projects.

Digital Story Creation

Android

Com-Phone Story Maker [free] combines audio, photos, and text to create stories while allowing for three different layers of audio.

WeVideo [free] is a web-based video editor that can mix images, text, video, and audio.

iOS

30hands [free] creates a story by adding narration to photos.

Magisto [free] uses a wizard to create a short video based on provided images or video content.

Splice [free/paid] combines photos, videos, music and narrations. Effects and transitions can be added.

WeVideo [free] is a web-based video editor that can mix images, text, video, and audio.

Computer

iMovie [paid] provides video creation and editing software that can create easily shareable content on a Mac. An iOS version is available.

Microsoft Photo Story 3 [free] for Windows lets you create slideshows from a wizard that includes audio, narration, and images.

Windows Movie Maker [free] for Windows operating systems is a video editing software application that allows for narration, audio, images, and video to be mixed and edited, and it comes with transitions and special effects.

Web

Animoto [paid] allows users to submit songs, choose a theme, add their photos, videos, and text to create a digital story that they can share.

Meograph [free] is a digital storytelling tool that relies on Google Earth to create map-based and timeline-based narrated stories.

WeVideo [free] is a web-based video editor that can mix images, text, video, and audio.

Image Resources

Android – n/a

iOS – n/a

Computer – n/a

Web

Cagle Cartoons [free] provides access to a number of political cartoons from around the world. The images are organized by topic with artists categorized by country.

Flickr Creative Commons [free] provides images that can be used for almost any educational project, as long as proper citation is followed

FreeFoto.com [free] has a photos area that is available under three licensing options: recognition, Creative Commons, and commercial.

Morguefile [free] provides a range of images that are copyright free, and are available for use with few or no restrictions.

Pics4Learning.com [free] is a website that provides safe and free images for educational uses. Images here are copyright-friendly and can be used for classrooms, multimedia projects, websites, videos, portfolios, or other projects.

PicSearch [free] allows you to search the internet for images, but be aware that the image may not be copyright-free, or that it may require permission to be used in projects or in any other educational contexts.

The Library of Congress Prints & Photographs Online Catalog [free] makes an attempt to ensure that as many of their images as possible are available online in a digital format.

Wikimedia [free] serves as a point from where all the images and video posted in Wikipedia can be viewed. Most of the images found here are either copyright-free or free for use with minimal restrictions.

Image Editing

Android

PicSay [free] can edit photos, overlay titles, and add special effects.

FX Camera [free] is a photo booth app that allows users to add various effects to photographs.

iOS

PhotoPad [free] can create, edit, and save vector illustrations. It can also work with photo library images.

ScreenChomp [free] allows you to share, explain, and markup images.

Computer

PhotoPad [paid] is an image editor for OS X.

PaintShop Pro [paid] is a comprehensive image editing package for Windows.

Web

Adobe Photoshop CC [paid] is a comprehensive cloud-based image editing package.

Phixr [free] is an online photo editor with various filters and effects, and it can connect to various social media sites.

FotoFlexer [free] is an online image editor offering a number of effects, distortions, and other features.

Pixlr [paid] is a comprehensive online photo editing app.

Interactive Whiteboards

Android

ExplainEverything [free] allows users to share their content by using an interactive screencasting whiteboard.

Interactive Whiteboard [free] is a virtual whiteboard that can be used for drawing or teaching various concepts as it allows for multiple finger input, straight line drawing mode, drawing move mode, and various other features.

PPT and Whiteboard Sharing [free] provides a way to share presentations, videos, and drawings in various settings including the classroom, the boardroom, and online meetings.

Whiteboard: Collaborative Draw [free] is a collaborative drawing application that allows real-time painting.

iOS

Doceri [trial/paid] combines screencasting, desktop control, and an interactive whiteboard in one application, with control through Airplay or through Mac or PC.

Educreations Interactive Whiteboard [free] is an interactive whiteboard and screencasting tool that allows annotation, animation, and narration of a number of content types.

Screenchomp [free] allows users to annotate pictures or to use the application as a whiteboard. Any work completed with the application can be saved automatically to the internet.

ShowMe Interactive Whiteboard [free] allows voice-over recording of whiteboard interactions so that tutorials can be created easily before being shared online.

Computer

Open Sakore [free] is open-source and it is dedicated to teacher and student use. It allows for insertion of multiple document types, along with annotation capabilities for commenting drawing and highlighting content.

Smoothboard Air [free] is a collaborative interactive whiteboard for multiple iPads and for Android tablets. It allows users to annotate desktop applications wirelessly through the use of a web browser.

Web

A Web Whiteboard [free] is a online whiteboard application that allows a number of devices (like computers, tablets, and smartphones), to draw sketches, and to collaborate with others around the globe.

Realtime Board [free] is a whiteboard in a browser that allows for collaboration among a number of users.

Twiddla [free] is a web-based meeting environment that allows users to mark up photos, graphics, and websites, or to just start out with a blank canvas.

Web Whiteboard [free] is a simple way to draw and write together online by creating an online whiteboard with a click, and sharing it live or by sending the link to others.

Mashups

Android

Edjing 5 DJ Music Mixer [free] not only transforms any android device into a turntable, but it provides access to a range of music libraries.

iOS

iMashup [paid] is a professional quality remixing app that allows users to create their own mashups and remixes.

Pacemaker [free] allows users to create and save mixes on an iPhone or iWatch, and to DJ live from iPad devices.

Computer

Mixxx [free] is an advanced open source DJ package that includes an extensive array of features for OS X and Windows.

Web

Mashstix [free] is a website with user submitted mashups available.

Media Timelines

Android

RWT Timelines [free] allows students to create a graphical representation of any event or process by displaying items sequentially along a line. The final product can be exported as a pdf, or saved to the device's camera roll.

Timeline [free] allows users to create timelines and associate them with colors, and to view multiple timelines together. It is a useful reference tool for remembering dates.

iOS

TimelineBuilder [paid] allows users to create custom timelines with images and text with unique beginning and end dates.

Timeline Maker [free] provides an easy way to display a series of events in a chronological order.

Computer

Edraw Timeline Maker [paid] is a tool that makes it simple to create a professional looking timeline, history, schedule, time table, or project plan diagram from scratch.

TimelineMaker [paid] provides a simplified timeline charting tool aimed at project planners, and business professionals, and those in educational contexts.

Web

Capzles [free] allows users to create rich multimedia experiences from videos, photos, music, blogs, and documents by integrating these into a timeline of sequential events, and then share them on various social media platforms.

Hstry [free] is specifically designed for the education sector, and it allows teachers and students to create interactive timelines for assignments and online sharing.

OurStory [free] offers a means for creating story-based timelines with pictures.

Timeline [free] from *readwritethink* allows students of all ages to easily create a graphical representation of related items or events in sequential order and display them along a line using various images and text.

TimeGlider [free] is a web-based timeline project creator that allows zooming and panning across timelines. Users are able to set the size of events as they relate to importance.

Tiki-Toki [free/paid] is a web-based timeline editor that allows viewing of timelines in 3D, and it allows for the integration of images and videos.

WhenInTime [free] is a web application for creating and sharing media-based timelines.

Music Resources

Android .

> *FindSounds* [free] can be used to search the internet for sounds that can then be saved as ringtones, notifications, or alarms.

> *Shazam* [free] allows Android device users to identify the music playing around them, as well as discover song lyrics, and other music related information and tracks.

iOS

> *Shazam* [free] allows iOS device users to identify the music playing around them, as well as discover song lyrics, and other music related information and tracks.

Computer – n/a

Web

> *300 Monks* [free] provides a comprehensive source of royalty free music.

> *ccMixter* [free] is a free music site that is community based and promotes a remix culture. *A cappella* and remix tracks licensed under Creative Commons are available for download and use in creative works.

FMA (Free Music Archive) [free] provides access to a range of free music based on a wide variety of genre. The music is offered free under various licenses for use.

Find Sounds [free] is a long-running service that can be used to search the internet for various sounds that can then be incorporated into various projects.

FreePlay Music [free] is a service that searches the internet for free music that can be used in YouTube videos and other projects.

Podcasting

Android

Podomatic Podcast & Mix Player [free] provides access to a wide variety of podcasts, listening in offline mode, and features such as a dynamic social feed so you can see the podcasts Facebook friends follow and like.

iOS

PodOmatic Podcast Player [free] provides access to a wide variety of podcasts, listening in offline mode, and features such as a dynamic social feed so you can see the podcasts Facebook friends follow and like.

Computer

Audacity [free] is a free multi-track audio recorder and editor with some very powerful features that include those for adding effects to files and conducting analysis of the audio recorded.

iTunes [free] offers media on demand and a way to organize and enjoy music, movies, and TV shows, as well as accessing and subscribing to podcasts and screencasts.

LoudBlog [free] is a Content Management System (CMS) for podcasts. This program automatically generates skinnable websites and RSS-feeds for audio and video podcasts, including provision for show notes and links.

PodcastGenerator [free] is an open source content management system for podcast publishing. It provides a comprehensive range of tools to manage all aspects of podcast publishing.

PodProducer [free] allows for the recording of voice and the adding of effects.

Web

ESLPod [free] provides a range of podcast content tailored to second-language learners of English from specific topics through to test-taking guides.

FeedForAll [free] allows for the creation, editing, and publishing of RSS feeds.

Feedity [free] is an online tool for creating an RSS feed for any web page, with an option to upgrade to a premium account that offers additional features.

FETCHRSS: RSS Generator [free] is an online RSS feed generator, that can create a feed out of almost any web page, automatically updates the RSS feed when new content is added to the web page, and generates an RSS for a social networking site.

OPML Viewer [free] allows users to view the contents of outline processor markup language (OPML) files.

Podcast Alley [free] is the place to go if you are interested in podcasts, want to gain access to the top podcasts, and want to find out the latest news about podcasts.

Pod Gallery [free] is a podcasting website where podcasters can share their episodes, and where listeners can subscribe.

QT-ESL Podcasts [free] provides a range of podcasts that cover oral grammar practice and includes scripts and worksheets.

SoundCloud [free] is a social sound platform where anyone is able to create and share audio.

Podcatchers

Android

Podcast Player [free] provides a range of podcast discovery options and tools, along with a range of features including a sleep timer, video support, intelligent silence skip and volume boost, as well as support for tablet, Chromecast, and Android Wear.

Podcast Republic [free] is an application that is ad-supported. It offers a variety of features from podcast discovery and automatic downloading through to storage management, sleep timer, and car mode. Support is also included from Chromecast and Android Wear.

Pocket Casts [paid] shows subscribed podcasts in a tile format, with easy sorting and categorization functions. Video podcast is also supported, along with auto-download and cleanup of downloaded and played episodes to save on storage space. Several features allow it to stand out, including a sleep timer as well as its cross-platform nature that grants it the ability to sync between multiple devices and mobile operating systems.

iOS

Overcast: Podcast Player [free] provides a combination of powerful audio and podcast management features. The application comes with a wide variety of features that allow it to download episodes, send notifications of new episodes, and play content offline or by streaming. It can also normalize speech levels, and speed through gaps and silence in podcasts.

Castro: High Fidelty Podcasts [free] is a simple and easy to use podcatcher. It provides a simple design with automatic episode download, dynamic storage management, along with episode streaming.

Pocket Casts [paid] shows subscribed podcasts in a tile format, with easy sorting and categorization functions. Video podcast is also supported, along with auto-download and cleanup of downloaded and played episodes to save on storage space. Several features allow it to stand out, including a sleep timer as well as its cross-platform nature that grants it the ability to sync between multiple devices and mobile operating systems.

Computer

gPodder [free] is an open source media aggregator and podcast client. It is able to store information in the cloud on which shows you have listened to, and it allows for the local installation of the client for download of content.

iTunes [free] is a comprehensive media aggregator that provides comprehensive support for media management, the audio and video playback of local media, podcast search and subscription, along with automatic downloads, syncing and streaming, and many other features.

Juice [free] is a long-standing cross platform no-frills podcast aggregator that is open source, and specifically designed to manage podcasts. Features include auto cleanup, centralized feed management, and for Windows users, accessibility options for the blind and visually impaired.

Web

Cloud Caster [free] is a web-based podcaster which works across all mobile devices. It syncs progress and playlists across platforms, and provides search and support for audio and video podcasts.

Presentations

Android

Glogster [free] allows students using an Android-based device to create online multimedia posters, or Glogs, from a combination of media types (from audio, graphic, to video), and hyperlinks.

Google Slides [free] allows Android device users with a Google account a means of creating, editing, and collaborating with others on presentations.

LinkedIn SlideShare [free] allows Android device users the ability to search and explore for a variety of presentations, infographics, and documents on topics of their interest.

Microsoft PowerPoint [free] allows users to view PowerPoint presentations on their device for free, and to make edits and changes on the go.

iOS

Glogster [free] allows students using an iOS device to create online multimedia posters, or Glogs, from a combination of media types (from audio, graphic, to video), and hyperlinks.

Google Slides [free] allows iOS device users with a Google account a means of creating, editing, and collaborating with others on presentations.

Keynote [free] is a powerful presentation app that allows users to develop comprehensive presentations with animations, transitions, and multimedia elements.

LinkedIn SlideShare [free] allows iOS device users the ability to search and explore for a variety of presentations, infographics, and documents on topics of their interest.

Microsoft PowerPoint [free] allows users to view PowerPoint presentations on their device for free, and to make edits and changes on the go.

Computer

Microsoft PowerPoint [paid] is a comprehensive presentation software application, and is perhaps the most used and recognizable.

Keynote [free] is a powerful presentation app that allows users to develop comprehensive presentations with animations, transitions, and multimedia elements.

Web

> *Bunkr* [free] is a presentation tool that displays any online content including social media posts, images, videos, audio, articles, and files.
>
> *Glogster* [free] allows students to create online multimedia posters, or Glogs, from a combination of media types (from audio, graphic, to video), and hyperlinks.
>
> *Google Slides* [free] allows those with a Google account, a means of creating, editing, and collaborating with others on presentations.
>
> *LinkedIn SlideShare* [free] allows users to search for presentations, infographics, documents and other items on topics of their interest.
>
> *Microsoft PowerPoint Online* [free] extends the Microsoft PowerPoint experience to the web browser with OneDrive integration, and allows users to create, edit, and view files on the go.
>
> *Prezi* [free] is a visually oriented presentation packaged that also allows users to upload PowerPoint slides, and customize them, or use a variety of their own images, text, audio, and video.

Slidebean [free] offers a one-click presentation development system that incorporates a variety of templates into the design of presentations.

Slides [free] is a place for creating, presenting, and sharing slide decks.

Swipe [free] allows users to share a presentation link with anyone across any device, and it allows viewers to interact with the presentation on several levels, from collaboration through to taking polls.

VoiceThread [free] allows users to import various media such as images, PowerPoints, and PDFs. It provides a means of making audio or video recordings concerning those media artifacts, and it also allows other users to reply to the initial comments, by audio or video means, as the presentation progresses.

Publishing

Android

Book Creator Free [free] offers a simple means of creating a variety of ebooks including picture books, comic and photo books, and journals and textbooks. It allows for the use of images, narration, texts, annotations and drawings.

Book Writer Free [free] is a simple book creation application that allows users to share their content with others.

My Story Builder [free] is a simple, 'suitable for children', book editor.

Scribble: Kids Book Maker [paid] is an application that allows children to write, illustrate, and publish their own comprehensive stories in a range of formations including video export. It contains a series of story starters, stickers, and backgrounds to help them work on creating stories from the start.

iOS

Book Creator Free [free] offers a simple means of creating a variety of ebooks including picture books, comic and photo books, and journals and textbooks. It allows for the use of images, narration, texts, annotations and drawings.

Creative Book Builder [paid] is a professional ebook editor and generator which can also extend the utility of ebooks through the use of a range of widgets.

Demibooks Composer Pro [free] builds interactive books with animation, audio, images, and effects.

Scribble Press – Creative Book Maker for Kids [paid] contains a series of story starters, stickers and backgrounds to help get young kids working on creating stories that can be turned into ebooks.

Computer

Android Book App Maker [paid] provides users with the ability to turn content into a flip-book app.

iBooks Author [free] provides a series of templates and styles to assist in the development of ebooks for the iBook store.

Kotobee [free] provides free software to assist in the creation of ebooks and libraries for a range of platforms.

Web

Blurb [paid] is just one of many online services that can assist in the creation of ebooks.

QR Codes

Android

I-nigma QR & Barcode Scanner (free) is a versatile barcode and QR code reader that can scan a multitude of codes and share these codes as well.

QR Code Reader (free) is a simple QR Code and product barcode scanner.

QR Droid Code Scanner (free) is a powerful barcode, QR code, and Data Matrix scanner that offers multi-language support.

iOS

Bakodo – Barcode Scanner and QR Barcode Reader (free) scans all types of QR codes and barcodes.

QR Reader for iPhone (free) scans a variety of codes including QR codes and barcodes, and features auto-detect scanning.

QRafter – QR Code and Barcode Reader and Generator (free) is a two-dimensional barcode scanner for iOS. Along with a variety of useful features, it can scan and generate QR codes.

Computer

CodeTwo QR Code Desktop Reader (free) allows users to scan QR codes directly from their screen onto their desktop. Users select the QR code to be read by selecting the area with a QR code using their mouse.

QR-Code Studio (free) is for Mac and Windows computers. The QR code maker software is freeware.

Web

QR Code Generator (free) creates QR codes, in a limited number of formats, for free.

QR Stuff QR Code Generator (free) creates QR codes from a various types of data such as website URLs, image files, PDF files, and so on, with static and dynamic embedding options.

The QR Code Generator (free) allows for the free scan and generation of QR codes for a variety of uses.

Rubrics

Android

Daily Rubric: Any Curriculum [free] allows teachers to create and use rubrics from their Android device. Rubrics can be designed from curriculum outcomes, or based on the pre-loaded Common Core Standards.

iOS

Easy Assessment [paid] offers a means to capture and assess performance based on custom created rubrics, scale, or criteria.

Rubrics [paid] allows instructors to track student performance and produce reports based on custom rubrics and grading options.

Computer – n/a

Web

Kathy Shrock's Guide to Everything: Assessment and Rubrics [free] provides access to a wide range of rubrics to help guide assessment of students.

iRubric [free] is a website where instructors can create their own rubrics, or they can build off those made available from other instructors.

RubiStar [free] allows instructors to create their own rubrics using templates designed for core subjects as well as art, music, and multimedia.

Screencasting

Android

AZ Screen Recorder [free] is a screen recording application that offers several features, including the ability to capture the front camera as well as screen recording. It also provides video trimming.

ilos Screen Recorder [free] is a simple application that records the screen and provides audio capture as well.

Telecine [free] is an open source application that allows screen recording through the use of overlays.

iOS

Doceri [trial/paid] combines screencasting, desktop control, and an interactive whiteboard in one application, with control through Airplay or through Mac or PC.

Educreations Interactive Whiteboard [free] is an interactive whiteboard and screencasting tool that allows annotation, animation, and narration of a number of content types.

Screenchomp [free] allows users to annotate pictures or to use the application as a whiteboard. Any work completed with the application can be saved automatically to the internet.

Computer

ilos screen recorder [free] automatically uploads content to their servers for storage and playback.

Screencast-O-Matic [free] offers fifteen minutes of recording time for free, both for screen and webcam, and allows users to save to places such as YouTube or as a video file.

TechSmith Camtasia Studio [free trial] is a comprehensive screen recording application that allows for audio and webcam capture as well as highlighting, adding media, and editing of recordings.

Web – n/a

Storyboarding and Scripting

Android

Ray Story Board [free] is a simple storyboard creator that lets users build storyboards from photos or gallery images, create multiple storyboards, and animate them using a slideshow feature.

Storyboard Studio [paid] is a mobile storyboarding writing tool that is suitable for artists and non-artists alike.

iOS

Penultimate [free] provides a natural feel of writing and sketching on paper, and connects to Evernote.

Storyboard Composer [paid] is a mobile storyboard previsualiztion composer for animators, art directors, film students, film directors, or anyone who would like to visualize their story.

Computer

FrameForge Previz Studio [paid] allows users to develop and previsualize films, TV shows, commercials, or similar projects at a professional level.

Storyboardpro [paid] is professional level software that combines drawing and animation tools with camera controls.

StoryBoard Quick Studio [paid] allows for the fast creation of storyboards with QuickShots, has a print-to-sketch feature, and comes with a series of character poses for integration into storylines.

Web

Google Docs [free] can be used, along with any note-taking or document editor, as a make-shift storyboard by integrating photos or pictures into the document to outline a process or the actions for a story. It is also available as an Android and iOS app.

StoryboardThat [free trial] offers an edition that allows educators to build diagrams, and visualize workflow. It features a drag and drop interface and an extensive image library.

Story Creation Apps

Android

StoryMaker 1 [free] provides a means of creating stories using templates and overlays, and the possibility of using audio, photos, or video.

Storehouse [free] allows users to share a collection of photos in a collage or album, or by telling a story that links the photos.

iOS

StoryKit [free] allows for the creation of an electronic storybook through the use of images, simple drawings, recording of sound, and by the addition of text.

Storyrobe [paid] makes photo-based slideshows with voice recording.

FotoBabble [free] adds audio to a photo to make a talking postcard.

Sock Puppets [free] lets users create lip-synced videos with characters. Various puppets, props, scenery, and backgrounds can be used.

Computer

Cartoon Story Maker 1.1 [free] is a simple program that creates 2D cartoon stories with conversations, dialogs (recorded and/or speech bubble), and various backgrounds.

StoryMaker [free/trial] is game-based software that asks for parts of speech (such as nouns, verbs, adjectives), and these are then inserted into a story with sometimes comical results. Educators can edit and customize aspects of the aspects of the program for their context. Backgrounds can be imported, but character templates are built in.

Web

Littlebirdtales [free] provides younger learners the ability to create digital storybooks.

Pixton [free/paid] is a visual writing tool that allows users to make a comic using images, clipart backgrounds and artwork, as well as speech bubbles.

Storynet.org [free] is a website that aims at connecting people to and through storytelling.

StoryJumper [free] allows users to create illustrated storybooks from scratch or from existing templates.

Video Editing

Android

VideoShow – Video Editor [free] is an all-in-one video editor and slideshow producer that provides music, themes, filters, emojis, as well as text input.

VidTrim [free] is a video editor and organizer that allows the trimming, editing, and saving of videos.

VivaVideo: Free Video Editor [free] is a comprehensive video editor and movie maker that facilitates the creation of video-based stories.

WeVideo [free] is a comprehensive and easy to use video editor that can mix images, text, video, and audio.

iOS

iMovie [paid] is video creation and editing software that can create easily shareable content.

Splice [free] is a video editor that adds music and effects to images and videos with narration. It includes access to free songs, sound effects, text overlays, transitions, filters, and various editing tools.

ReelDirector II [paid] is a full-featured video editing app.

WeVideo [free] is an easy to use and comprehensive video editor that can mix audio, images, text, and audio.

Computer

Windows Movie Maker [free] is a video editing software application that allows for narration, audio, images, and video to be mixed and edited with transitions and special effects.

Web

Video Toolbox [free] is an online video editing and conversion tool.

WeVideo [free] is a comprehensive and easy to use web-based video editor that can mix images, text, video, and audio together to form a compelling story.

Video Resources

Android

TED [free] provides more than 2,000 TED talks from various people by topic and mood, and on a variety of topics.

Vimeo [free] is a variety of videos are available across a wide variety of topics and genres, with users having the ability to upload their own content as well.

YouTube [free] allows for editing and uploading of videos, where one can subscribe to various channels that offer a wide variety of videos on various topics and genres.

iOS

TED [free] provides more than 2,000 TED talks from various people by topic and mood, and on a variety of topics.

Vimeo [free] provides a variety of videos which are available across a wide variety of topics and genres. Users are able to upload their own content as well.

YouTube [free] allows for editing and uploading of videos, where once can subscribe to various channels that offer a wide variety of videos on various topics and genres.

Computer – n/a

Web

Clipcanvas [free] allows for the download of 600,000 royalty free HD and 4K video and film clips.

Mazwai [free] maintains a collection of free to use HD video clips and footage, and some unique time-lapse and slow motion video footages that are provided under the Creative Commons Attribution license if used commercially.

Motion Backgrounds for Free [free] is a place to download professional quality motion backgrounds and video footage.

Motion Elements [free] is a good source for premium stock videos, offering around 400 videos for free, as well as free After Effects templates.

Neo's Clip Archive [free] offers nearly 3,500 free video clips sorted by 25 categories free for use for personal, non-commercial purposes.

Pexels Videos [free] brings under one roof a video library of Creative Commons Zero licensed stock videos from a variety of different sources.

SaveTube [free] allows users to rip YouTube videos to their local computer in various audio or video-based formats.

Savevideo.me [free] allows users to rip videos from a variety of sites to their local computer.

TeacherTube [free] is an online resource that helps users to view and share videos, photos, audio, and documents on almost any topic.

WebQuests

Android – n/a

iOS – n/a

Computer – n/a

Web

> *Building a WebQuest* [free] is a comprehensive overview of the template to follow when there is a need to construct a WebQuest.
>
> *Having Fun with Reading* [free] is a WebQuest for college and adult level learners of English, where learners interact with texts and complete activities that promote cooperative and collaborative learning along with reading narrative comprehension skills.
>
> *Idioms in Your Pocket* [free] is a WebQuest that is designed for high school and adult ESL students, and it allows them to discover the various meanings of English idioms.
>
> *OneStopEnglish WebQuests* [free] provides a selection of WebQuests covering major holidays.
>
> *Pre-Writing Your WebQuest* [free] provides prompts for users to complete in order to develop a WebQuest.

QuestGarden [free/paid] is a site designed by Bernie Dodge, the creator of WebQuests, for use by pre- and in-service teachers, professional developers, other educators, and those who work with them. The site provides hosting and template creation of WebQuests that then become searchable.

Using WebQuests to Teach English [free] is a WebQuest that can be used to teach teachers about WebQuests.

WebQuestDirect [free] is described as the world's largest searchable directory of WebQuest reviews.

WebQuest.Org [free] provides comprehensive information pertaining to the WebQuest model, and is run by Bernie Dodge, the creator of WebQuests.

Zunal [free/paid] is a site for educators to create, host, and then share their WebQuests with others.

Wikis
Android

EveryWiki: Wikipedia++ [free] aims to provide access to many wikis from a central application.

wikiHow [free] is the application associated with the leading how-to-guide wikiHow. It allows for searching of the wiki to find step-by-step instructions on how to complete almost any task.

iOS

Hack My Life – Life Hack Wiki [free] is an application that seeks to provide access to all possible life hacks. A life hack is a strategy or technique that can be used or adopted to allow for better time management or for getting more out of everyday activities.

Lyrically [free] offers access to a list of song lyrics curated by fans. Searches can be undertaken by track, artist, or by song, and there is support for in-app purchases.

Computer

DokuWiki [free] is a PHP based highly customizable and fully extensible wiki software platform. The advantage is that it requires no databases as all the data is stored in plain text, and for this reason, it is very popular and used by many sites. It has a variety of useful features, from locking to avoid edits through to a spam blacklist.

MediaWiki [free] is open-source and it is the wiki software used by Wikipedia. It is available in a number of languages, released under a general public license (GPL), and written in PHP: Hypertext Preprocessor (PHP) a server-side scripting language. There are many extensions and plugins available for free, including a what-you-see-is-what-you-get (WYSIWYG) editor.

Web

PBworks [free] (formerly PBwiki) is a real-time collaborative editing system with several solutions including one for educators. It offers a single workspace, where student accounts can be created without email addresses, and easy editing without the need for coding.

PmWiki [free] is a wiki tool that gives user-access control over individual pages, so they can be set for access by specific people with it being possible to set different passwords for each page. The software also allows for navigation trails through individual sections, insertion of tables, and provides a printable layout.

Wikidot [free] offers members the ability to create a wiki-based website with forums, where they can create a community, or publish and share documents and content.

Wikispaces [free] is a wiki hosting service that provides educators with a means to monitor student progress in real time and the ability to easily create projects and assign them to students, as well as editing tools and a social newsfeed.

Teacher Notes

Android

_____

_____

_____

_____

_____

_____

_____

_____

_____

_____

_____

_____

_____

_____

_____

_____

_____

_____

_____

_____

_____

_____

_____

iOS

_____

_____

_____

_____

_____

_____

_____

_____

_____

_____

_____

_____

_____

_____

_____

_____

_____

_____

_____

_____

_____

Computer

_____

_____

_____

_____

_____

_____

_____

_____

_____

_____

_____

_____

_____

_____

_____

_____

_____

_____

_____

_____

_____

Web

_____

_____

_____

_____

_____

_____

_____

_____

_____

_____

_____

_____

_____

_____

_____

_____

_____

_____

_____

_____

_____

_____

16
References

Ahmad, S. Z. (2012). The effect of WebQuests on EFL students' critical reading. *First International Conference of the Egyptian Association for Curriculum and Instruction.* September 5-6. Suez, Egypt.

Alshumaimeri, Y. A., & Almasri, M. M. (2012). The Effects of Using Webquests on reading comprehension performance of Saudi EFL students. *TOJET: The Turkish Online Journal of Educational Technology, 11*(4), 295-306.

Arauz, P. E. (2013). Inquiry-based learning in an English as a foreign language class: A Proposal. *Revista De Lenguas Modernas,* 19. 479-485.

Benjamin, J. Y. (2003, January 08). A checklist for evaluating WebQuests. *Tech & Learning.* Retrieved from http://www.techlearning.com/news/0002/a-checklist-for-evaluating-webquests/55765

Chou, I. C. (2014). Situated learning: Learn to tell English stories. *Journal of Education and Training Studies, 2*(4), 113-118.

Chuo, T. W. I. (2007). The effects of the WebQuest writing instruction program on EFL learners' writing performance, writing apprehension and perception. *TESL-EJ, 11*(3), 1-27.

Croome, J. (2011). *12 easy steps to the making of a book trailer*. Retrieved from http://www. thebookdesigner.com/2011/05/12-easy-steps-to-the-making-of-a-book-trailer/

Dodge, B. (2001). Five rules for writing a great WebQuest. *Learning & Leading with Technology, 28*(8), 6-9.

Dodge, B. (2015). *What is a WebQuest?* Retrieved from http://webquest.org

Doyle, B. (2015). *How to create an Animoto book trailer*. Retrieved from https://www.youtube.com/watch?v=mUWjNHs7c5c

EBC (2004). *Concept to classroom*. Retrieved from http://www.thirteen.org/edonline/concept2class/webquests/index.html

FMA. (2016). *free music archive*. Retrieved from http://freemusicarchive.org/

Goins, J. (2016). *Why most book trailers are awful and how yours can be different*. Retrieved from http://goinswriter.com/book-trailer

Harclerode, M. (n.d.). *Book trailers for readers*. Retrieved from http://www.booktrailersforreaders.com/How+to+make+a+book+trailer

JLG (2016). *What makes a good book trailer*. Retrieved from https://www.youtube.com/watch?v=wYQCaolRQ4g

Koenraad, T.L., & Westhoff, G. J. (2003). Can you tell a LanguageQuest when you see one?: Design criteria for TalenQuests. *Conference of the European Association for Computer Assisted Language Learning*. September 3-6. University of Limerick, Ireland.

Kocoglu, Z. (2010). WebQuests in EFL reading/writing classroom. *Innovation and Creativity in Education, 2*(2), 3524-3527.

Lincoln, L. (2014). *Book trailer tutorial using (Windows) Movie Maker*. Retrieved from https://www.youtube.com/watch?v=t9e-4xumP4A

March, T. (2004). New needs, new curriculum. *Educational Leadership, 61*(4), 42-47.

Matsil, N. (2015). *How to make a book trailer for free (That looks professional).* Retrieved from https://www.powtoon.com/blog/book-trailer-free-professional/

Mazwai. (2016). *Mazwai.* Retrieved from http://mazwai.com

Najafi, S. (2013). *Fantastic book trailers and the reasons they are so good.* Retrieved from http://therumpus. net/2013/06/fantastic-book-trailers-and-the-reasons-theyre-so-good/

Pederson, R. (2013). Situated learning: Rethinking a ubiquitous theory. *The Journal of Asia TEFL,* 9(2), 123-148.

Penn, J. (2013). *Book Trailers: 11 Steps to make your own.* Retrieved from http://www.thecreativepenn.com/2008/12/03/book-trailers-11-steps-to-make-your-own/

Penn, J. (2015). *Book trailers and using video for book marketing.* Retrieved from http://www. thecreativepenn.com/2015/03/02/book-trailers/

Plickers. (2016). *Tailor instruction with instant feedback.* Retrieved from http://plickers.com

Prapinwong, M., & Puthikanon, N. (2008). An evaluation of an internet-based learning model from EFL perspectives. *Asian EFL Journal, 27,* 1-50.

Sambuchino, C. (2016). *How to make a book trailer: 6 steps.* Retrieved from http://www.writersdigest. com/editor-blogs/guide-to-literary-agents/how-to-make-a-book-trailer-6-tips

Schiller, M. (2015). *Spotlight on business: 4 elements of an awesome Animoto book trailer.* Retrieved from https://animoto.com/blog/business/animato-book-trailer/

Tech4Learning, Inc. (2016). *Pics4Learning.* Retrieved from http://pics4learning.com/

WikiHow. (2016). *How to do a presentation in class.* Retrieved from http://www.wikihow.com/Do-a-Presentation-in-Class

Zlatkovska, E. (2010). Webquests as a constructivist tool in the EFL teaching methodology class in a university in Macedonia. *CORELL: Computer Resources for Language Learning 3,* 14-24.

About the Book

With an increasing need to teach multiple literacies, WebQuests are as relevant today as they were at the dawn of the internet. They are adaptable to student needs as well as the curriculum, and they allow teachers to create material that focuses on student development in engaging and motivating ways that can, in turn, inspire collaboration, creativity, and linguistic development. Extremely student-centered but teacher guided, WebQuests offer access to authentic tasks through the use of a scaffolded learning approach based on constructivism and situated learning, and these tasks are completed through participation in an inquiry-based method. In this book, these pedagogical affordances are examined in light of the teaching of English to speakers of other languages (TESOL). Instructional strategies and activities along with tutorials on how to get started with WebQuests are included, along with photocopiable handouts and templates, evaluation techniques, and a comprehensive list of resources. Are you ready to take your students on the WebQuest of their lives?

About the Author

David Kent is an Assistant Professor at the Graduate School of TESOL-MALL at Woosong University in the Republic of Korea. He has been working and teaching in Korea since 1995, and with a Doctorate of Education from Curtin University in Australia, he is a specialist in computer assisted language learning (CALL) and the teaching of English to speakers of other languages (TESOL). He has presented at international conferences, as well as published a number of peer-reviewed journal articles, books, and book chapters in his areas of specialization.

Also by David Kent

A Loanword Approach to the Teaching of
English as a Foreign Language in Korea:
Exploring the Effectiveness of a Multimedia Curriculum

Teaching with Technology:
Integrating Technology into the TESOL Classroom

TESOL Strategy Guides
Digital Storytelling
The Prezi Presentation Paradigm
Podcasts and Screencasts
WebQuests